Air War over Syria

Tu-160, Tu-95MS & Tu-22M3

Cruise Missile and Bombing Strikes on Syria
November 2015-February 2016

HUGH HARKINS

Copyright © 2016 Hugh Harkins

All rights reserved.

ISBN: 1-903630-65-7
ISBN-13: 978-1-903630-65-5

Air War over Syria
Tu-160, Tu-95MS & Tu-22M3

Cruise Missile and Bombing Strikes on Syria
November 2015-February 2016

© Hugh Harkins 2016

Published by Centurion Publishing
United Kingdom

ISBN 10: 1-903630-65-7
ISBN 13: 978-1-903630-65-5

This volume first published in 2016
The Author is identified as the copyright holder of this work under sections 77 and 78 of the Copyright Designs and Patents Act 1988

Cover design © Centurion Publishing & Createspace

Page layout, concept and design © Centurion Publishing

All rights reserved. No part of this publication may be reproduced, stored in a retrieval system, transmitted in any form, or by any means, electronic, mechanical or photocopied, recorded or otherwise, without the written permission of the Publisher

The Publisher and Author would like to thank all organisations and services for their assistance and contributions in the preparation of this volume: Tupolev PJSC, UAC (United Aircraft Corporation), JSC Tactical Missiles Corporation, JSC Concern Radio-Electronic Technologies (KRET), Rostec Corporation and the Ministry of Defence of the Russian Federation

CONTENTS

	INTRODUCTION	i
1	THE SYRIAN WAR – RUSSIA'S OPENING MOVES	3
2	LONG RANGE AVIATION'S CRUISE MISSILE CARRIER/BOMBER TRIAD – Tu-160, Tu-95MS & Tu-22M3	13
3	LONG RANGE AVITION CRUISE MISSILE/BOMBING CAMPAIGN OVER SYRIA – NOVEMBER 2015-FEBRUARY 2016	41
4	APPENDICES	77
5	GLOSARY	80

INTRODUCTION

The primary remit of this volume is to document the cruise missile and long range bombing missions flown by the Tupolev Tu-160 & Tu-95MS strategic cruise missiles carrier aircraft and the Tu-22M3 long-range bombers of the Russian Federation Aerospace forces Long Range Aviation against Islamic State and other opposition groups in the Syrian conflict. A secondary remit is the documentation of the cruise missile strikes carried out on targets in Syria by the Russian Federation navy.

While the volume is not intended to be a descriptive manual for the three missile carrier/bomber types portrayed, a basic description of the genesis, development and fielding of these weapon systems is provided in chapter two. Chapter three focuses mainly on the missions flown by Long Range Aviation during its campaign over Syria between November 2015 and February 2016.

It is beyond the remit of this volume to attempt a detailed analysis of the Syrian conflict, which was in its fifth year before the Russian intervention in 2015. That said, a brief outline of the situation on the ground in certain areas is provided where appropriate to the Russian campaign as well as a brief outline of the differences in the Russian and western dominated anti-ISIS coalition approach to the attempt to defeat ISIS forces, which, in early 2016, continue to dominate the majority of the land of Syria.

All technical information concerning aircraft and weapons, along with the majority of the graphic material, has been furnished by the respective manufacturers and the MODRF.

1

THE SYRIAN WAR – RUSSIA's OPENING MOVES

On 23 December 2015, whilst Russia was embroiled in an on-going air campaign over Syria, Russian Long Range Aviation, an element of Russia's Aerospace Force, celebrated its 101st anniversary. At this time the striking force consisted of Tupolev Tu-95MS strategic cruise missile carriers, Tupolev Tu-160 strategic cruise missile carrier/strategic bombers and Tupolev Tu-22M3 long-range bomber/missile carriers. These were supported by a handful of Tu-22MR long-range reconnaissance aircraft, Antonov A-30B 'Special Purpose Aircraft', for reconnaissance, Ilyushin Il-78M air refueling tanker aircraft, Antonov An-12 and Antonov An-26 transport aircraft and Russian Helicopters Mi-8 and Mi-26 transport helicopters.

Completely distinct from Long Range Aviation, the Russian Federation Navy also possessed a long range cruise missile conventional strike capability in the shape of its surface warship and submarine launched Kalibr cruise missiles.

The Russian campaign in Syria had commenced on 30 September 2015, when, in response to a request for assistance from the government of the Syrian Arab Republic, the Aerospace Group, which had been forming at Hmeymin air base over the previous few weeks, formally commenced combat operations against ISIS (Islamic State) and other groups it deemed to be terrorist organisations embroiled in the Syrian civil war. A side issue leading to the Russian intervention was the threat of mission creep by the US-led anti-ISIS coalition then conducting air strikes, mainly against ISIS forces opposed to the so called moderate opposition backed financially and to a certain degree with armament supplies by the coalition and other partner nations. However, the main aim of the anti-ISSI coalition and other countries such as the United Kingdom, appeared to be the overthrow of the Syrian President, Bashar Al Assad, the threat of extending airstrikes to Syrian government forces embroiled in the fight against ISIS being ever present, as was the threat of a ground invasion; the presence of Russian forces fighting alongside Syrian government forces would, it was clear, to all intents and purposes remove this threat. Russia, for its part, saw the preservation of the Assad regime as the surest way to defeat ISIS on the ground in Syria, there being no other alternative as the 'moderate opposition' forces lacked the capability for such a campaign. Even supported by air power from the anti-ISIS coalition, the moderate opposition was, for the most part, coming up wanting when faced with determined opposition from ISIS forces. Their inability to contribute significantly to the offensive fight against ISIS, combined with their operations against government forces, which succeeded in drawing government forces away from the fight against ISIS, caused no little annoyance in Russia, which held the view that such groups were part of the greater extremist threat to Syria.

The Tu-22M3 would become Long Range Aviation's main strike asset in its campaign over Syria between November 2015 and February 2016. UAC

Even prior to the Russian intervention on 30 September 2015, the western powers had lost any initiative they thought they had in Syria; ISIS appearing to be all advancing. While voices in Washington and London were outspoken against Russia's position from the start, the Russian operation had much support throughout the world, but more importantly it had almost overwhelming support from those countries bordering or near to Syria, which would be most affected by an ISIS controlled Syria. Iraq, embroiled in its own fight against ISIS, gave permission for Russian aircraft to overfly its territory on ferry and transport flights to Syria as well as strike missions by aircraft emanating from Russia and cruise missiles launched from Russian warships cruising in the Caspian Sea or launched from Russian aircraft within Iranian airspace. Israel tacitly supported the operation, knowing all too well that, in the current climate, the only viable alternative to the Assad regime in Syria was an Islamic State that would be anything but friendly to Israel. Jordan supported the operation, going on to host a coordination centre for Russian Syrian operations in Amman. Egypt expressed its support for the operation and the UAE (United Arab Emirates), which was operating as part of the anti-ISIS coalition, embraced the Russian operation as that nation and Russia both opposed a common enemy – ISIS. In the immediate region, Turkey and Saudi Arabia expressed hostility to the Russian operation, Saudi Araba's statements sounding like they could have been scripted in London or Washington, the United Kingdom and United States outspoken comments against Moscow being to a large extent outshone by the outright hostile comments and actions of Turkey towards the Russian operation.

The main striking power employed over Syria would be the tactical combat aircraft of the Russian Aerospace Group, Sukhoi Su-24M and Su-34 strike aircraft, Su-25SM ground attack aircraft and Su-30SM multirole strike fighters, all based at Hmeymim air base, western Syria. As the campaign progressed, these in theatre assets would be reinforced with additional Su-34's, and, from early February 2016, a small detachment of Su-35S $4^{th}++$ generation multirole strike fighters; these latter aircraft assumed to have been deployed to counter the potential air threat inherent within the NATO command structure, particularly from Turkey.

The Russian air strikes were conducted within the Syrian command structure, a joint Russian/Syrian command centre being located at Hmeymin air base to this end. In the first days of the campaign the MODRF (Ministry of Defence of the Russian Federation) stated that Russian aircraft were only assigned targets that were "outside inhabited areas", these targets being attacked only once their validity had been confirmed by reconnaissance and other intelligence sources. The main reconnaissance tools at their disposal being in the shape of space based satellite reconnaissance and UAV (Uninhabited Air Vehicles), some 70 of the latter stated to have been operational in Syria by the end of February 2016.

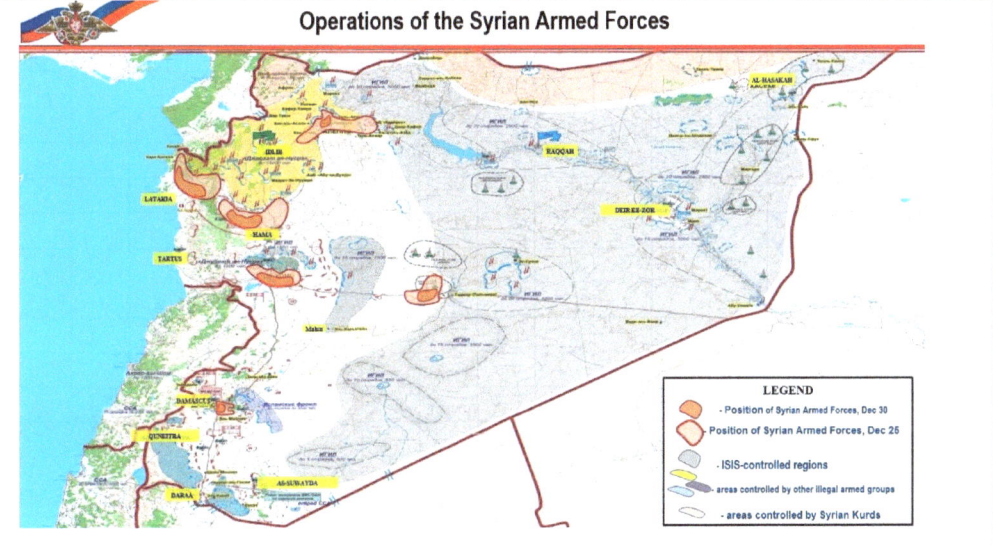

Chart showing the land mass controlled by different groups in the last week or so of December 2015. As can be seen, ISIS controlled almost all of central and eastern Syria save a few hold outs such as Dier ez Zor, which would become a focus of Long Range Aviation's bombing effort. MODRF

Previous page: The Russian Aerospace Group based at Hmeymim air base, Syria, included a quartet of Su-30SM 4th+ generation multifunctional 'super-manoeuvrable' strike fighters (top) and Su-25SM ground attack aircraft (bottom). This page: The main strike elements of the Russian Aerospace group based at Hmeymim was the updated Sukhoi Su-24M strike aircraft, one here dropping unguided bombs on a target in Syria (top) and the modern 4th+ generation Su-34 strike aircraft seen landing at Hmeymim (above). MODRF

Two graphics depicting the Kalibr cruise missile which is available in 3M-14 submarine launched and 3M-14T ship launched variants. MODRF and NPO Saturn

Also at the disposal of the Russian Federation political and military command structure from day one was air and naval strike assets not in theatre, not least of which was the Kalibr-NK cruise missiles carried by Russian submarines and surface warships and air launched cruise missiles, including the Kh-101, carried by the Tu-160 and Tu-95MS strategic missile carriers as well as the striking power provided by Long Range Aviation's Tu-22M3 long range bomber Divisions.

The Russian Navy Caspian Flotilla cruises to its firing point in the Caspian Sea (top) and launches the first salvo of cruise missiles at targets in Syria on 7 October 2015 (above). MODRF.

The seeds of the first cruise missile strike on Syria were sown on 5-6 October 2015, when, according to the reports of the Chief of the Main Operational Directorate of the General Staff of the Russian Armed Forces, Colonel General Andrei Kartapolov, a number of key, apparently time critical, targets had been located by reconnaissance assets. Following verification of the validity of the intelligence data using services of Russian, Syrian, Iranian and Iraqi organisations, it was decided, in accordance with Russia's stated aim of increasing the tempo of its strike operations, particularly against ISIS and Jabhat al-Nusra groups, to employ cruise missiles, agreement being reached for overflights by the "Russian partners", as stated by the MODRF.

3M-14T Kalibr cruise missiles illuminate the missile ship of the Caspian Flotilla from which they are being launched. MODRF

The task of conducting the cruise missile attack was allocated to the Russian Navy Caspian Flotilla, which is the maritime element of the Russian southern military district. The weapon of choice being the 3M-14T ship-launched variant of the Kalibr cruise missile which has a range of around 2000 km and can be armed with either nuclear or conventional warheads, only the conventional armed variant of course being considered for strikes on targets in Syria.

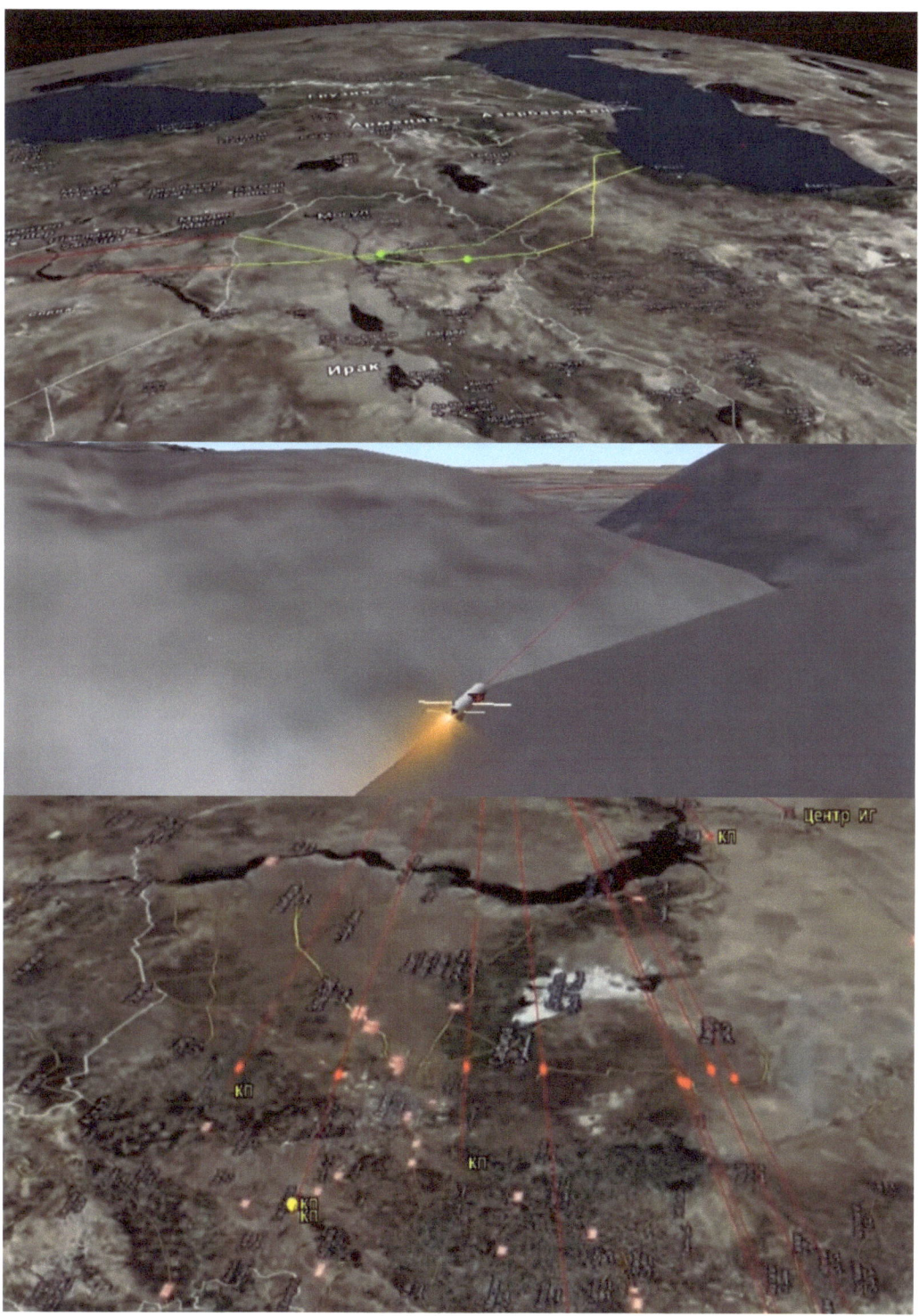

Graphics depicting the 7 October cruise missile attack on Syria showing the missiles flight path, yellow lines through Iran and Iraq and red lines through Syrian airspace (top), a missile during terrain following flight (centre) and the terminal phase of the attack in Syria (bottom). MODRF

The Kalibr, which is also available in a submarine launched variant – 3M-14, cruises in complex flight profiles to the target at altitudes down to about 30 m, the missile having an accuracy stated as approximately 5 m, the target being destroyed by a 500 kg class high explosive warhead.

During the pre-dawn hours of 7 October 2015, twenty six 3M-14T Kalibr missiles were launched form the Caspian Flotilla small missile ships *Dagestan*, *Grad Sviyazhsk*, *Veliky Ustyug* and *Uglich* cruising in the South West area of the Caspian Sea. As far as can be ascertained the missiles made landfall on the Iranian southwestern Caspian coast and continued on a southwesterly course before turning easterly and crossing over Northern Iraq before entering Syrian airspace and proceeding to their targets, described by Kartapolov as "plants producing ammunition and explosives, command centres, storages of munitions, armament and POL as well as training camp of terrorists", all targets being in the Raqqah, Idlib and Aleppo regions.

As the campaign progressed, although Russia continued with a high tempo of air operations out of Hmeymim air base, it looked like the 7 October cruise missiles strikes would be an isolated incident. However, going into November, in the wake of the bombing of a Russian civilian Airbus A321 airliner over Egypt on 31 October 2015, in an act of terrorism that killed 224 people, responsibility of which was claimed by ISIS, the Russian high command was looking at options for, at least temporarily, increasing the tempo of combat operations without the requirement to provide large scale air asset reinforcements to the Russian Aerospace Group operating a mix of tactical combat aircraft types, out of Hmeymin. To this end, in mid-November 2015, the Supreme Commander-in-Chief of the Russian Armed Forces formally issued instructions for increasing the level of combat operations over Syria, with a not insignificant percentage of strikes to focus on the illegal oil producing and distribution activities of ISIS, which Russia made great pains to point out was being transported out of Syria more or less without hindrance through northern Iraq and Turkey.

The Russian high command decided that its best course of action was to call on the long range strike assets of Long Range Aviation which began preparing to fly missions direct from Russian territory, employing Tu-160 and Tu-95MS cruise missile carriers and Tu-22M3 long-range bomber/missile carriers, a major effort being planned for the 17th of the month, augmenting the efforts of tactical aviation based at Hmeymim which had already intensified its operations against oil targets, including road convoys of tankers in transit. Russia's decision to focus attention on reducing the flow of oil, which it stated was financially benefiting Turkey, would increase the already strained relations with its southern NATO neighbour, which retained the tacit political support of its NATO partner nations, despite the embarrassment of the portrayal of collusion with the ISIS illegal oil trade. This support was by no means replicated by the general populations of NATO countries, much of which was already averse to Turkeys hardline approach to civil rights taken for granted within the European Union and North America, It appeared clear, as part of its military campaigns against its own Kurdish populations, Turkey had certain territorial ambitions in northern Syria.

2

LONG RANGE AVIATION'S CRUISE MISSILE CARRIER/BOMBER TRIAD – Tu-160, Tu-95MS & Tu-22M3

In the half decade or so leading up its late summer 2015 intervention in the Syrian War, the Russian Federation Air Force, forming a part of the Russian Aerospace Force from 1 August 2015, had begun to revitalise itself from an inefficient underfunded organisation equipped with an aging fleet of combat aircraft, mostly dating back to the late 1970's, 1980's and early 1990's, into an efficient professional combat arm of the Russian Federation, progressively re-equipping with new $4^{th}+/4^{th}++$ generation aircraft able to rival, and in many areas, surpass the capability of their NATO opposite numbers. In 2016, the service was preparing to enter the realm of 5th generation combat aircraft with the delayed delivery of the first few Sukhoi T-50 PAK FA (*Perspektivniy Aviacionniy Complex Frontovoi Aviacii* – Perspective [Prospective] Aviation Complex for Front line Aviation) 5th generation multifunctional 'stealth' fighter aircraft expected to enter service in 2017. A new stealth optimised bomber program – the PAK DA (Perspective [Prospective] Aviation Complex for Long Range Aviation) – is currently planned to fly in 2019, with deliveries to Long Range Aviation (LRA) – the strategic missile carrier/bomber force – scheduled for 2023.

While looking to the future and the PAK DA, Long Range Aviation embarked upon modernisation programs for its current fleet of Tu-160 and Tu-95MS strategic missile carrier and Tu-22M3 long-range bomber/missile carrier aircraft to keep them viable as strike platforms until new bombers become available in the 2020's, under current planning. In addition to the modernisation programs, plans are underway to re-introduce the Tu-160 to production status, although the resultant Tu-160M2 will be equipped with new fifth generation avionics and weapons control systems under development for the PAK DA; the program, in addition to increasing the numbers of airframes in the Tu-160 fleet, providing a viable option as a strategic cruise missile carrier/bomber to fall back on in the event of the PAK DA program cancellation.

Tupolev's cruise missile carrier/bomber trio of Tu-95MS (front), Tu-160 (centre) and Tu-22M3 (upper left of photograph) in company with Tupolev's current (2016) stable of civil airliners. Tupolev

The modernisation of the Russian cruise missile carrier/bomber triad provided a quantum leap in capability through new avionics and weapons, the latter including the much vaunted JSC Tactical Missiles Corporation (JSC Raduga State Engineering Design Bureau) Kh-101 and Kh-102 cruise missile family, the former armed with a conventional warhead and the latter armed with a nuclear warhead. These highly capable weapons, designed for very low observability in the radio contrast, visible light and infrared spectrums, have a stated flight range of up to 4500 km, providing Russia with an air launched stand-off conventional and nuclear strike capability unrivalled by any other nation.

The importance of Long Range Aviation to the Russian Federation cannot be overstated. The force, neglected for so long during the post-Soviet years of austerity in the 1990's and through much of the first decade of the 21st century, is viewed as a symbol of national pride, the most visible element of the Russian nuclear deterrent triad which also consists of ground (silo and mobile) launched ICBM (Inter Continental Ballistic Missiles) and submarine launched SLBM (Submarine Launched Ballistic Missiles). Long Range Aviation, although an element of the Aerospace Forces, remains distinct from tactical and army aviation, coming under the direct command of the Supreme Commander-in-Chief of the Armed Forces of the Russian Federation.

This Tu-95MS strategic missile carrier, RF-94130, was photographed by an RAF Eurofighter Typhoon of No.6 Squadron operating on QRA out of RAF Leuchars, Scotland. Crown Copyright

Having undergone a number of changes in recent years Long Range Aviation is currently organised under the Air Base command structure. As far as can be ascertained the strike element consists of four bomber divisions, although this may be as high six, the uncertainly surrounding whether or not each of the Tu-22M3 Regiments is administered under a separate divisional structure. The division based at Engels (Saratov), which was for many years known as the 22nd Guards Heavy Bomber Division, but now known under the banner of the 6950th Guards Air Base, is equipped with two Heavy Bomber (Cruise Missile Carrier) Regiments, namely the 121st Guards Regiment equipped with the Tu-160 and the 184th Guards Regiment equipped with Tu-95MS. The Ukrainka (Amurskaya) based 79th and 182nd Guards Regiments, both equipped with Tu-95MS, come under the organisation of the 6952nd Air Base, which was formerly known as the 326th Heavy Bomber Division.

Following the reorganisation of the Russian Air Forces into the Aerospace Forces, information on the permanent bases of the Tu-22M3 divisions, prior to reorganisation these including the 52nd, 200th, 326th and 840th Heavy Bomber Regiments, has proved harder to confirm than those of the other elements of LRA. What is known is that the four Tu-22M3 long range bomber Regiments come under the organisational command of the 6953rd Air Base (Belaya air base), apparently located at Srednil, Irkutsk, Oblast. Tu-22M3 units, however, are often forward deployed, in recent years to the Crimea – annexed by Russia in 2014 following a referendum by the population of Crimea – and of course Mozdok in North Ossetia.

The bomber force is supported by the Il-78M in-flight refueling tanker aircraft, these apparently operated by the 203rd Regiment which is normally based at Ryzazan, but may well come under the operational control of the 6950th Guards Air Base.

As conceived, designed and built, the Tu-95MS, allocated the NATO reporting name 'Bear' H, was to be the main element of the Soviet and later Russian air launched strategic nuclear deterrent armed with Kh-55 (X-55) air launched cruise missiles, which, like the carrier aircraft, entered service in the 1980's. Crown Copyright

For many the first impression on viewing the Tu-95MS is that it appears to be a metachronism, a Cold War relic of a bygone era. However, this is merely an illusion, the Tu-95MS being a highly capable intercontinental cruise missile carrying strategic strike aircraft, the main element of Long Range Aviation's nuclear deterrent capability armed with stand-off cruise missiles – Kh-55 and Kh-102 with a secondary conventional role armed with conventional armed cruise missiles.

In terms of basic flight performance, the turboprop powered Tu-95MS has a speed only some 70 or so km/h less than that of the jet powered Boeing B-52 strategic bomber in service with the USAF, which in terms of operational airframes is considerably older than the Tu-95MS fleet, the latter entering service only in the 1980's, deliveries continuing into the early 1990's. The basic Tu-95 design is, however, as dated as that of the B-52, the prototype of the initial Tu-95 design, '95/1', flying for the first time on 12 November 1952, the same year as the YB-52.

The basic design of the Tu-95 (remaining the case for the current Tu-95MS) was a normal aerodynamic configuration featuring, as stated by Tupolev, "a high-lying cantilevered three-spar wing", which proved to be aerodynamically efficient when flying at high speeds, the Tupolev description reading "This aerodynamic design provides high aerodynamic efficiency at high speed flight." Tupolev continued, "Aircraft performance improvement is also achieved by a high aspect ratio wing, corresponding to the angle of its sweep and a set of profiles along the span."

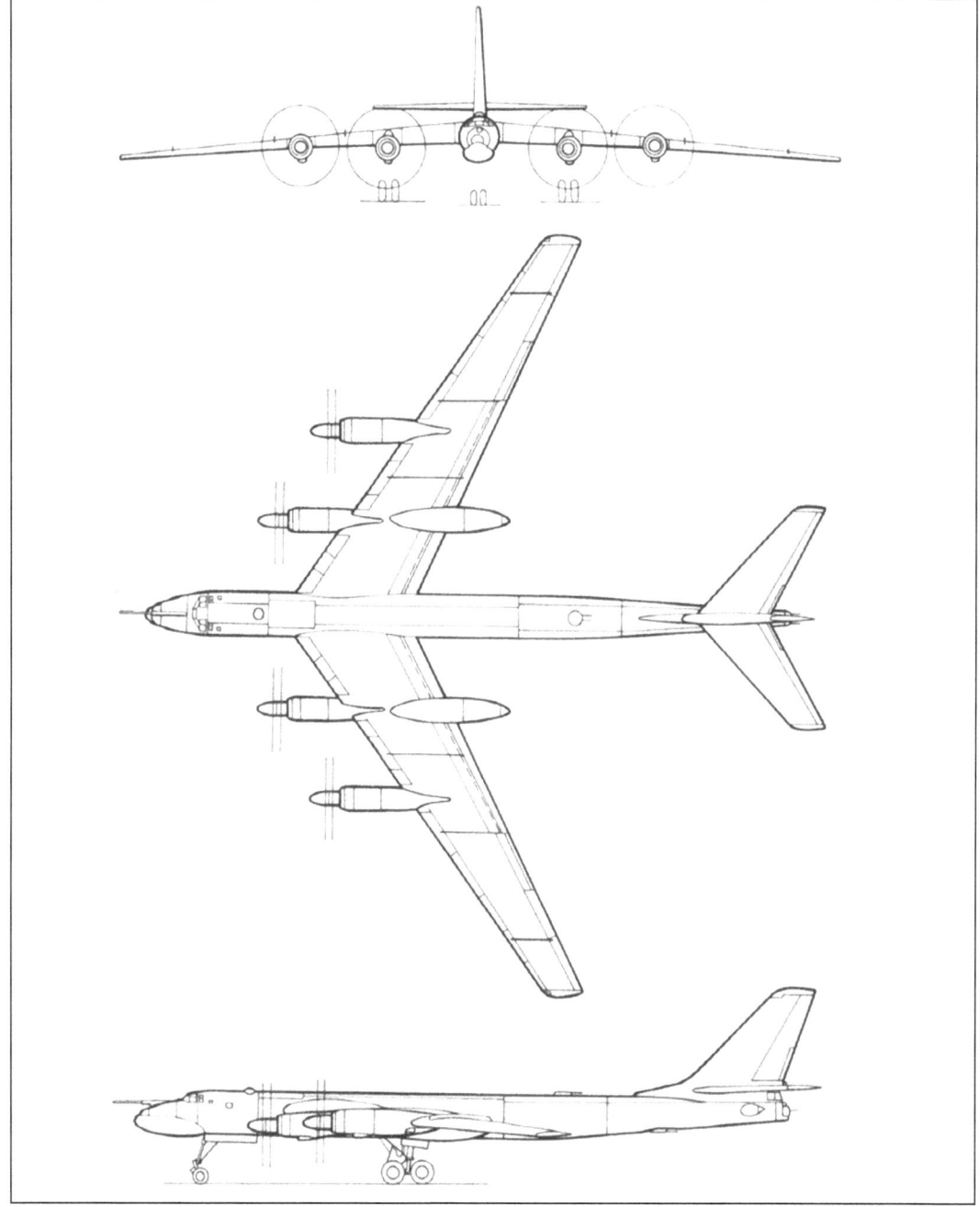

Three-view general arrangement drawing of the Tu-95MS cruise missile carrier. UAC

The 4 x NK-12 turboprop engines, designed by N. Kuznetsov, drive AB-60K coaxial (contra-rotating) four bladed propellers (designed by K. Zhdanov), the engines, each of which generate 15,000 hp, being fed by fuel housed in a central fuselage fuel tank and two central and four integral wing fuel tanks, refueling being centralised. In the Tu-95MS range can be extended through in-flight refueling courtesy of a fixed in-flight refueling probe located on the upper nose section.

Top: The Tu-95MS is powered by 4 x NK-12 turboprop engines driving four-blade contra-rotating propellers. Above: The primary sensor is the Obzor-MS long-range pulse-Doppler navigation and attack radar housed in the nose section. UAC and Tupolev

Serial production of the first generation Tu-95 commenced in 1955, the first operational variants entering Soviet service in 1957, with several hundred aircraft being manufactured in a plethora of variants; bomber, missile carrier, long range reconnaissance, oceanic reconnaissance and other special purpose variants. Many of the first generation variants served into the 1980's, some Tu-95M's being converted to Tu-95U trainer configuration in which they served into the early 1990's.

The Tu-142 anti-submarine design, which conducted its maiden flight on 18 June 1968, was developed from the first generations Tu-95. This improved design would form the basis of the Tu-95MS strategic missile carrier armed with the X-55 (Kh-55) air launched cruise missile, which resulted from a drive to design a smaller, more compact, cruise missile for internal carriage by the Tu-95, the Raduga Machine Building Design Bureau, in the early 1970's, embarking upon the X-55 program under the design leadership of General Designer I. Seleznev.

It was proposed than a modernised variant of the Tu-142M, designated Tu-142MS (later Tu-95MS), would be developed as the new missile carrier, work on this variant commencing in July 1977 with the converted Tu-142M being complete by September 1979, conducting its maiden flight as the Tu-95MS prototype that month.

Following a test program, production of the Tu-95MS commenced at Taganrog aircraft production plant in 1981 before being transferred to Kuibyshev (now Samara) during 1983, production continuing until early 1992.

Following the break-up of the Soviet Union in 1991, long-range patrols by aircraft of Long Range Aviation all but ceased. However, in August 2007, such patrols were reconstituted in order to show a Russian presence in such areas as the North Atlantic and North Pacific regions as Russia increasingly began to feel threatened by an expanding NATO presence on her borders. UAC

The Tu-95MS is equipped with a Leninets Obzor-MS long-range pulse-Doppler navigation and attack radar system, located in the aircraft nose section. This radar system, allocated the NATO reporting name 'Clam Pipe', has undergone updates that apparently include a SAR (Synthetic Aperture Radar) capability and DBS (Doppler Beam Sharpening) modes for increased ground mapping resolution. As the Tu-95MS was designed to fly cruise missile attack profiles at medium altitudes there was no requirement for a TFR (Terrain Following Radar) capability.

The self-defence and ECM (Electronic Counter Measures) suites include an SPS-171/172 electronically steerable phased-array jamming system, this being part of the overall Avtomat RWR (Radar Warning Receiver) system. Other elements of the suite include a SPS-160 Geran active jammer, an Azovsky MAK-UT(L) L-082 IR (Infrared) MAWS (Missile Approach Warning System) and Avtomatika SPO-32/L-150 digital warning receiver, all of which are integrated with the Meteor-NM EWSP controller. The disposable element of the self-defence system consisted of an APP-50 chaff/flare dispenser system. The hard kill element of the self-defence suite consisted of a GSh-23 23 mm cannon system housed in the tail position, the Tu-95MS design having discarded the gun barrets of previous generation Tu-95's.

Air launched cruise missiles for use on Tu-95MS and Tu-160 strategic missile carriers during maintenance or assembly. JSC Tactical Missiles Corporation

For its primary nuclear strike role the Tu-95MS is armed with the Kh-55 or Kh-102 air launched cruise missile, six of which are carried on and launched from a SRPE MKU-5-6 rotary launcher located in the internal weapons bay. While six is the maximum number of Kh-55 missiles that can be carried by the Tu-95MS-6, a further ten such missiles can be carried on under wing stations on the Tu-95MS-16. In the conventional long-range stand-off strike role the nuclear armed missiles are replaced by conventional armed missiles like the Kh-101, which is apparently more or less identical to the Kh-102 with the exception that the nuclear warhead in the latter is replaced by a 500 kg class (possibly larger) high explosive warhead in the former.

Page 22-23: Tu-95MS during modernisation and on being redelivered post modernisation in 2015-2016. Most of the aircraft appear to be Tu-95MS-6, but the aircraft at the bottom of page 22 is a Tu-95MS-16, recognisable by the external stations for the carriage of cruise missiles beneath the inner wing sections. Tupolev and UAC

In the second decade of the 21st century the Russian operational fleet of Tu-95MS aircraft stood at 28 Tu-95-6 and 35 Tu-95-16 aircraft, as fleet was about to embark upon an update program, part of a wider program to upgrade much of Long Range Aviation's Tu-95MS, Tu-160 and Tu-22M3 cruise missile carrier/long range bomber fleet. In regards to the Tu-95MS this included replacing the electronic equipment and improving the aircraft targeting capabilities, intended to keep the aircraft current until 2025 when it is hoped the PAK DA would be available. Modernisation of the Obzor-MS radar system, as is the case with the Obzor-K radar system installed in the Tu-160, are aimed at providing not only increased targeting and navigation capabilities, but also a reduction in detectability, being informally referred to as low probability of intercept enhancements, although it is unclear to what extent the radar modernisation has been implemented in the systems installed in the modernised Tu-95MS and Tu-160.

By 14 December 2015, eight or nine modernised Tu-95MS had been redelivered to Long Range Aviation, that service expecting to receive around 20 such aircraft by the end of 2016.

Referred to in Russian Federation Long Range Aviation service as an Intercontinental Strategic Multi-Mode Missile Carrier designed to strike high value installations on intercontinental deep penetration missions, the Tu-160 possesses enormous combat potential in both nuclear and conventional long-range strike scenarios armed primarily with air launched cruise missiles.

A US intelligence agency artist impression from the early 1980's showing a Tupolev Tu-160 undergoing arming with cruise missiles being loaded onto a rotary launcher in an internal weapons bay. US DoD

Possessing an unquestionable outward resemblance to the American Rockwell (later Boeing) B-1 strategic bomber, the Tu-160, being the heaviest combat aircraft ever built, is not only larger than the B-1, but possess far greater performance, particularly in such areas as kinetics, maximum speed being around 400 km/h faster than the B-1B. The Tu-160 ceiling is also considerably greater than that of the American aircraft, these values being 14000 m and 9140 m respectively (Tupolev and Boeing figures). Unrefueled range of the Tu-160, stated as 14000 km, is also considerably greater than that of the B-1B.

Comparisons with the B-1 are dismissed among elements of the Tu-160 design team, the Russian aircraft, as noted above, being much larger and possessing very different performance parameters, Tupolev stating it was more advanced and ultimately more capable than the American aircraft. Certainly in regards to airframe and flight performance this would ring true. However, the B-1B has benefited from huge sums being spent on avionics and weapon capability upgrades, most recently incorporation of the B-1B IBS (Integrated Battle Station), making it probably the most versatile of the US bomber triad, with a diversity of weapons able to be employed. That said, the Tu-160, with its 4000+ km range Kh-101/Kh-102 cruise missiles, possesses a stand-off strike capability that cannot be rivalled by any other aircraft, except perhaps the much slower turboprop powered Tu-95MS described above, which in its Tu-95MS-16 form can carry four missiles more than the Tu-160.

Known affectionately in Russian service as the 'White Swan', the Tu-160, allocated the NATO reporting name 'Blackjack', represents the pinnacle of current (2016) Russian long range airborne strike capability. Tupolev

Design work on the new Soviet supersonic bomber commenced at Tupolev Design Bureau in the early 1970's, the basic design concept being settled on by the middle of the decade. The Tu-160 design is described by Tupolev as being built on "a low faired scheme with a variable swept back wing, tricycle landing gear, all moving stabilizer fin", and all moving horizontal stabilizers. The control surfaces on the variable-geometry wings include slats, double-slotted flaps (for roll control and guidance) and drooped ailerons. As the wings are swept backwards boundary layer fences are raised from the inner part of the variable sweep wings improving lift and drag ratios, particularly in the fully swept back, 65°, position. The airframe is constructed mainly of titanium, steel alloys, heat-treated aluminium alloys and composite materials.

The Tu-160 is powered by four NK-32 turbofan engines grouped in two's in nacelles located in two pods mounted on the underside of the fixed wing sanction, these being the most powerful engines ever fitted to a combat aircraft, with a thrust rating of 25 tons (~22680 kg) in afterburner, giving a combined thrust for the four engines of 100 tons = more than 90700 kgf. Variable geometry ramps in the engine intakes optimise airflow to the engines during various parameters of flight, bestowing upon the Tu-160 its 1800 km/h speed flight performance (Tupolev value). A stand-alone TA-12 APU (Auxiliary Power Unit) provides power to aircraft systems independent of the engines while the aircraft is on the ground.

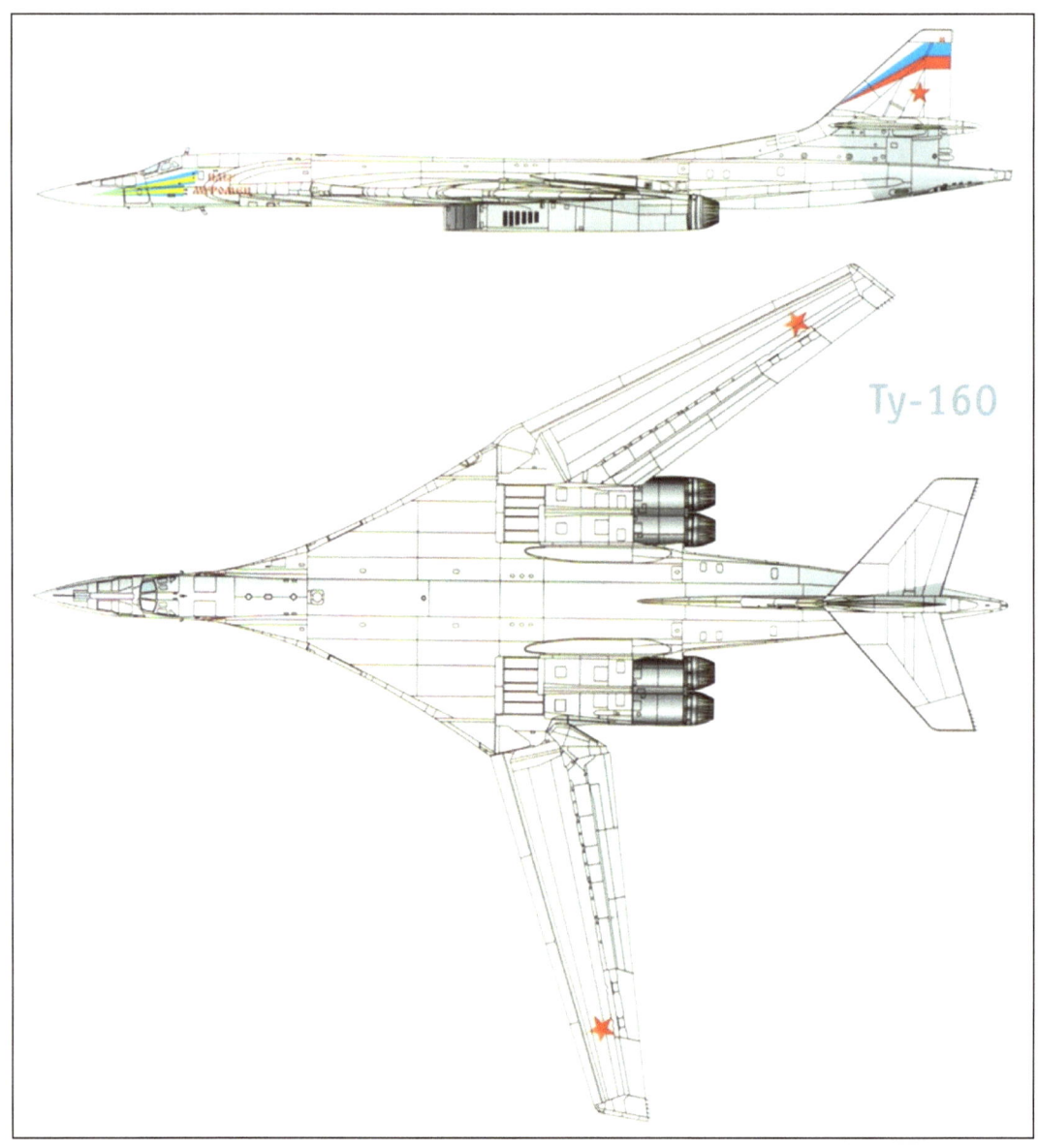

Two-view general arrangement drawing of the Tu-160. This graphic depicts the aircraft with its port wing in the forward (upswept) position and the starboard wing in the fully swept back position. UAV

Fuel tanks feeding the engines include two front fuselage/fixed wing section blend and one in rear fuselage, the three holding a combined total of 171 tons (various sources state conflicting figures, 171 tons being the upper value and 130 tons being the lower value) of fuel, bestowing upon the aircraft a very high unrefueled flight range. The already impressive range can be further increased by in-flight refueling courtesy of a retractable in-flight refueling probe mounted on the aircraft upper nose section.

The Tu-160 is powered by **4 x NK-32 afterburning turbofan engines providing a combined thrust in excess of 90700 kgf for take-off.** UAC

The primary sensor of the Tu-160 is the Obzor-K radar located in the aircraft nose section. The ventral fairing for the **OBP-15T** electro-optic bombsight is located below the cockpit area. The cockpit interior (above) is typical of a 1980's era combat aircraft design. Tupolev and Rostec Corporation

The aircraft interior accommodates a forward fuselage crew compartment with pilot and co-pilot seated side-by-side at the front and the navigator and defensive systems operator side by side behind, all crew being seated on K-36D zero zero ejection seats. Designed from the outset for extremely long-range flights, a toilet facility, kitchen and sleeping berths are provided for the crew.

On touch down during the landing process, three large braking parachutes are deployed from the rear nose cone. UAC

The primary targeting and navigation sensors include the nose mounted radar system, a modified variant of the Leninets Obzor-MS fitted in the Tu-95MS, designated Obzor-K, this variant being integrated with a Sopka terrain following radar, allowing the Tu-160 to fly low-level penetration missions if required. The Obzor-K range is around 300 km, the range of the Obzor-MS fitted in the Tu-95MS probably being only slightly different, if at all.

The Groza OBP-15T remote electro-optic TV sighing system, located in a ventral position on the forward fuselage, is designed for the employment of free fall unguided munitions. As well as radar and bomb-sighting systems the targeting system may include a SMKRITTs RORSAT, or equivalent, targeting datalink receiver (Molniya satcom) and an AFA-15 strike camera.

The navigation suite includes a satellite navigation system, originally an early system that pre-dated the Russian GLONASS and US NAVSTAR systems. Other elements of the navigation and communications suite are thought to be similar to the Tu-22M3, NK-45 navigation system, DISS-7 Doppler Navigation system, RV-5 low altitude altimeter, RV-18G radio altimeter, RSBN-PKV TACAN, R-832M UHF and R-847 HF systems; some navigation elements being integrated with the autopilot.

Towards the rear nose cone are elements of the self-defence suite designed for the detection and jamming of threat radar systems - the defensive systems may include an AG-65 ECM (Electronic Counter Measures) automatic noise generator, Avtomat-2 and 3 RWR (Radar Warning Receiver) for the detection of airborne radars, such as those carried by fighter aircraft and ground based radar systems respectively. At the extreme point of the tail cone is located the thermal detection system designed to detect threats such as missiles and aircraft in the rear hemisphere, this system thought to be along the lines of the L-082 MAK-UT(L) IR MAWS fitted in the Tu-95MS. The disposable element of the self-defence system consists of the APP-50 chaff/flare dispenser system, flare ejection bays being located on the rear fuselage lateral/undersides.

There are two large internal weapons bays, the doors for which open downwards and outwards from the fuselage underside. These can accommodate 22 tons of free fall munitions or a six round rotary launcher in each bay for an operational load of 12 x Kh-55SM/Kh-102 nuclear armed cruise missiles or Kh-101 conventional armed cruise missiles, the Kh-55SM having a flight range in excess of 2000 km while the Kh-102/Kh-101 have a flight range up to 4500 km.

Items of the radar detection and jamming elements of the Tu-160 self-defence suite are located at the rear of the aircraft, a major protrusion being on the same plane as that of the horizontal stabilizers. UAC

The prototype Tu-160 conducted its maiden flight on 18 December 1981, serial production commencing a few years later, the design entering operational testing in October 1984. The first operational Soviet Tu-160 unit was the 184th Bomber Regiment of the 37th Air Fleet, based at Priluky air base, Poltava Oblast, Ukraine, the first two aircraft arriving there on 17 April 1987. Initially it was planned for Soviet

Long Range Aviation to field up to 100 Tu-160's, but when the Soviet Union began to break-up in 1991, production had totaled only 35 airframes, some of which were incomplete, production continuing at drip pace in the 1990's, and, with the passing over into a new century a total of 36 Tu-160's had been built (this figure apparently including a single new-built aircraft delivered in the early 2000's).

The above figures, however, belied the numbers of such aircraft available for operations with the Russian Federation, which inherited Long Range Aviation, as 19 of the Soviet Union's 23 or so operational Tu-160 aircraft were inherited by Ukraine on the break-up of the Soviet Union in 1991. The Tu-160 aircraft remaining in Russia were allocated to the 121st Guards Heavy Bomber Regiment at Engels air base, Saratov, only six such aircraft being on strength by 1994, an insufficient number to constitute a viable strike force. Ten of the Ukrainian Tu-160's were scrapped, one went to a Museum, and the remaining eight were purchased by Russia in 1999, along with three Tu-95MS-16 and several hundred Kh-55 cruise missiles, under a contract valued at US $285 million, which was deducted from Ukraine's natural gas debt to Russia. The first of the ex-Ukrainian aircraft arrived at Engels on 6 November 1999, followed by the remaining seven over the next several months, Russia's fleet of such aircraft increasing to 16 by February 2001, air to air refueling training for the Russian Federation fleet of Tu-160's commencing that same year. Over the next few years the Tu-160 force worked up, being officially declared operational in Russian Federation Air Force Long Range Aviation service in 2005.

Going into 2016, the Russian Federation Air Force had a fleet of 16 Tu-160's, including a few modernised aircraft, the first of which was redelivered from the Kazan aviation plant on 19 December 2014, following the incorporation of an upgraded avionics suite that had completed bench testing on 25 March 2013.

The two large internal weapon bays can each accommodate a six round rotary launcher for the deployment of conventional or nuclear armed cruise missiles. Kret

Tu-160 ground operations at Engels air base in early 2016. UAC

The only weapon acknowledged by the MODRF as being employed by the Tu-95MS and Tu-160 on operations over Syria has been the modern Kh-101 low-observable air launched cruise missile. That said, media released by the MODRF appears to show at least two distinct types of missile. Very little is known about the Kh-101/102 missiles, the former armed with a conventional warhead and the later armed with a nuclear warhead, which are often simply described as modernised variants of the Kh-55 air launched cruise missile; the first launch of this latter weapon from Tu-160 taking place in June 1987. On analysis, however, the Kh-101, which apparently entered Long Range Aviation Service in late 2012, appears to be much more than simply an evolved Kh-55, range being more than doubled from the 2000 km of the Kh-55 to 4500 km, as stated by the MODRF.

Like the Kh-55, the Kh-101/102 are powered by a single turbofan engine located in the rear of the missile; this being extended below the missile just before launch. The small wings and tail surfaces do not deploy until after the missile has been released from the rotary launcher and drops away from the carrier aircraft.

In regards to the Kh-55, the missile follows a terrain following profile between 30 and 100 m from the Earth's surface, cruising at speeds of ~850 km/h. For over water operations an INS (Inertial Navigation System) guidance system is used. No details have been released on the guidance systems employed by the Kh-101/102, but these are likely to include a GPS (Global Positioning System) combined with a modern terrain following system.

The Kh-55 was designed to be hard to detect in the radio contrast spectrum, the low observable qualities of the Kh-101/102 being considerably enhanced over its forebear making the missile very difficult to detect and target in the visual, radio contrast and infrared spectrums.

In the Kh-55, as is likely the case with the Kh-101/102, targeting and terrain profile data was uploaded to the missile before it was loaded onto the launch aircraft. Once launched and on their way to the target, the missiles, launched in multiples of up to six, could change position regularly and even profile mask, by which one missile maneuvers behind the other to confuse detection radar systems and electro-optic systems. On nearing the target the missiles can spread out further and can attack from different directions.

A Tu-160 is shadowed by a RAF Panavia Tornado F.3 interceptor as it skirts the UK air defence identification zone in the UK area of interest. Encounters with NATO aircraft had increased in tempo for several years leading up to 2015. Crown Copyright

Although sharing the Tu-22 designation, the Tu-22M had little in-common with the first generation Tu-22 (above). Tupolev

The smallest and shortest legged of the Russian missile carrier/long range bomber triad, the Tupolev Tu-22M3, allocated the NATO reporting name 'Bakcfire' C, was designed as a supersonic strike bomber capable of attacking land and seaborne targets with free fall bombs and guided missile platforms. In regards to the latter, the Tu-22M3 took on the role of aircraft carrier killer, tasked with destroying NATO aircraft carrier battle groups in the event that the Cold War turned hot.

Although the designation would imply that the Tu-22M was a further development of the Tu-22, this is illusionary as the aircraft, as conceived, developed and built, was a completely new design, the Tu-22 designation being a necessity to court funding for the program in a time when ICBM (Intercontinental Ballistic Missiles) were favoured over strategic bomber aircraft by the Soviet political leadership.

Designed as a Tupolev Tu-16 replacement, the first generation Tu-22, '105 Project', was officially born on 15 August 1955, the prototype conducting its maiden flight on 21 June 1958. From 1959 until 1969, 311 Tu-22's were built in a number of variants including Tu-22A and Tu-22B bombers, Tu-22P Scout, Tu-22K missile carrier, Tu-22P jammer and Tu-22U trainer.

When design work commenced in 1965, without the benefit of state funding due to the aforementioned preference for ICBM's, the Tu-22M (Modernised) was initially known under the product code '145', with official designations of 'AM' and 'YN', the aircraft being touted as a profound modernisation of the Tu-22K. As the design progressed, the final product code '45' was applied and by 1967, with the engines mounted in the rear fuselage with the trunks on both sides of the aircraft keel, combined with the adoption of variable-geometry (swing-wings), any resemblance to the Tu-22K faded.

The early variants of the Tu-22M included the Tu-22M2, NATO reporting name 'Backfire' B, one here being shadowed by a USN Grumman F-14A Tomcat fleet air defence fighter. US DoD

A resolution of the Soviet government authorising a modification from the Tu-22K was issued on 28 November 1967, this design, to be powered by two NK-144-22 engines and referred to as the Tu-22KM, would become the Tu-22M powered by two NK-25 afterburning turbofan engines each rated 25000 kgf.

As designed, much of the Tu-22M flight and weapon deployment operations were automated., the aircraft being designed along the lines of a normal aerodynamic layout with a cantilever low-wing variable geometry wing configuration featuring a semi-monocoque fuselage which rests on a tricycle undercarriage system, the six-wheel main units of which retract to lie in the fixed inner wing section at the fuselage wing join; the twin-wheel nose unit retracting aft to lie in the forward fuselage underside. The airframe is built from mainly aluminum and steel alloys and some magnesium.

The wing consists of a fixed inner part and the variable-geometry section, which can sweep from 65° to 20°. Wing control surfaces consist of the flap system, including slats, three section double slotted flaps and three section spoilers, without ailerons. For roll control the spoilers are operated differentially and also double as airbrakes, the function of lateral control being preserved. The design incorporated a single vertical tail fin with all-moving stabilizer.

Page 36-37: Tu-22M3's of Long Range Aviation. UAC

The two NK-25 afterburning turbofan engines are housed side-by-side in the rear fuselage; variable-geometry air intakes feeding air to the engines through the above mentioned lateral fuselage mounted intake trunks. For ground operations power is supplied by an AP TA-6A Auxiliary Power Unit located in the dorsal fin.

The Tu-22M3 is equipped with a Leninets PNA-D attack radar, earlier variants of the Tu-22M being equipped with the PNA-A/B variants. This system can apparently perform the function of terrain following and Doppler beam sharpening ground mapping modes. A Groza OBP-15T remote TV sighing system is located in a ventral position on the forward fuselage, this system, which is designed for the employment of free fall unguided munitions, also being employed on the Tu-160, although visually the optics windows appear distinct. As well as radar and bomb-sighting systems, the targeting system includes a SMKRITTs RORSAT targeting datalink receiver (Molniya satcom) and an AFA-15 strike camera.

The communications and navigation suite, the latter integrated with the ABSU-145M autopilot, consists of the NK-45 navigation system, DISS-7 Doppler Navigation system, RV-5 low altitude altimeter, RV-18G radio altimeter, RSBN-PKV TACAN, R-832M UHF and R-847 HF systems.

The defensive systems include an AG-65 ECM automatic noise generator, Avtomat-2 and 3 for the detection of radar systems and an L-082 MAK-UL IR MAWS. The disposable element of the self-defence system consists of the APP-50 chaff/flare dispenser system while a hard-kill self-defence capability is provided by the GSh-23 23 mm cannon, with 1200 rounds of ammunition, housed in a barbette in the tail, apparently under the designation UKA-9A-802, this incorporating an upgraded PRS-4KM Kripton fire control and ranging/tail warning radar for the cannon and a TP-1 tail warning/fire control TV camera system.

Tu-22M3. Tupolev

With a maximum take-off weight of 124 tons, the Tu-22M3 has an impressive performance for an aircraft of its size, with a maximum speed of 2000 km/h, an operational ceiling of 14000 m and an unrefueled operational tactical range of 2200 km, this of course could be increased by the application of in-flight refueling courtesy of the retractable in-fight refueling probe located on the upper nose section.

Capable of carrying up to 24040 kg (53,000 lb.) of ordnance in the internal weapons bay and on external stores stations, the Tu-22M3's were tasked with a multitude of roles including anti-ship strike, nuclear strike and conventional bombing. The primary anti-ship weapon was the Kh-22, a single example of this large weapon being carried in a semi-conformal manner on the fuselage underside. A further two Kh-22 weapons could be carried on stations mounted on the in-board, fixed wing section; these stations alternatively being capable of carrying other munitions. For the nuclear strike role the Tu-22M3 can carry the Kh-15 short range nuclear tipped missile. In the conventional bombing role the Tu-22M3 is apparently capable of carrying up to 69 x FAB-250 series 250 kg class bombs or 42 x 500 kg weapons in the internal weapon bay and externally on multi-shackle racks, this being in excess of the number of 250 kg class weapons that could be carried by the considerably larger USAF B-52H, although the B-52H has a considerably longer range. Larger free fall weapons could be carried such as the FAB-1500 1500 kg class weapon, eight being the maximum load out.

While the FAB-250 series bombs appear to have been the standard weapon employed on operations over Syria, the normal load carried on missions appearing to be twelve such weapons, released video graphic material shows a Tu-22M3 dropping a single large weapon, presumably a FAB-1500 series weapon.

Top and above: Tu-22M3's being redelivered to Long Range Aviation following upgrade and overhaul at the Kazan production plant in 2015. Tupolev

The prototype Tu-22M0 had been manufactured by mid-1969, taking to the sky on its maiden flight on 30 August that year with test pilot V.P. Borisov as commander. The first Tu-22M3 conducted its maiden flight on 20 June 1977, and, following testing, the design was ordered into serial production in 1978, and, although having already been in service for several years, was officially declared operational in March 1989.

In all some 500 Tu-22M0/1/2/3 aircraft were built at the Kazan aircraft production plant. Exact number of Tu-22M3 built are hazy at best, but this is considered to certainly be in excess of 200, with estimates of around 250 considered plausible, production ending in 1993. Recent western estimates put the figure of operational Tu-22M3/MR (the Tu-22MR is a reconnaissance variant of the Tu-22M3, only a small number being built, the survivors remaining in Long Range Aviation service in 2016) at around 70, although it is clear that considerably more airframes are available, many being used for training and trials work and others being kept in various conditions of open storage. A number of the operational fleet have gone through a modernisation and overhaul program, with more aircraft being worked on as the 2015/2016 campaign over Syria progressed.

Long Range Aviation's Tu-95MS, Tu-160 and Tu-22M3 operations are supported by other assets including Long Range Aviation's Il-78M in-flight refueling tanker aircraft, apparently operated by the 203rd Regiment. This Il-78M is landing at Engels air base. UAC

3

LONG RANGE AVIATION CRUISE MISSILE/BOMBING CAMPAIGN OVER SYRIA – NOVEMBER 2015-FEBRUARY 2016

In the few years prior to 2015, Long Range Aviation had begun to reenergise itself as flying hours increased in training operations for both its primary nuclear deterrent role and the conventional strike role that would be demonstrated in the skies over Syria in late 2015 and early 2016. During the course of 2015, the assets of Long Range Aviation further increased the tempo of operations, flying patrols over several geographical areas including the North Pacific and North Atlantic Oceans. In addition to such routine operations, several major exercises were conducted, including Centre-15 and Combat Comonwealth-2015. Combat readiness inspections were also conducted as the proficiency of air and ground crew was increased. A number of cruise missile launches were undertaken by the strategic missile carrier Divisions, presumably JSC Tactical Missiles Corporation (JSC Raduga State Engineering Design Bureau) Kh-101 and or Kh-102 and Kh-55/Kh-55SM, as well as bombing missions against range targets by the Tu-22M3 Regiments.

Once the decision had been taken to employ the assets of Long Range Aviation in the Syrian campaign it was necessary to organise the necessary command structure. Operational control of the operations emanating from Russian territory would be administered from the Russian National Centre on State Control of the Russian Federation through the Long Range Aviation and the Russian Aerospace Group in Syria command and the various communications centres.

Long Range Aviation had a force of Tu-22M3 long-range bombers forward deployed at Mozdok air base near the town of Mozdok in the Republic of North Ossetia-Aliana, which lies some 92 km from Vladlkavkaz, the capital of North Ossetia-Aliana and some 2000 km or so from its intended targets in Syria.. This Tu-22M3 force was reinforced as preparations were made for operations over Syria, and through 16 November 2016, the Bomber Regiments at the base were prepared for the coming missions to be flown the following day. Aircraft were checked, fueled, bombs were loaded and crews were briefed.

Tupolev Tu-22M3 long range bombers at Mozdok air base, North Ossetia-Aliana, being prepared for operations over the Syrian Arab Republic on 16 or 17 November 2015. MODRF

There is a fair degree of ambiguity surrounding the Russian operations on 17 November, not least of which are the details surrounding the operations of the Caspian Flotilla. Russian reports of the day's operations omitted details of any Kalibr missile launches that day, however, operations charts clearly show at least two waves of Kalibr missiles striking targets in Syria, although the number of missiles are omitted. As best can be best ascertained form the conflicting information released by various MODRF (Ministry of Defence of the Russian Federation) sources, combined with operational charts released, it seems that the mornings operations consisted of pre-dawn air strikes by the tactical aviation based at Hmeymim on targets in eastern and northern Syria, followed by the first wave of Tu-22M3's which bombed targets in eastern Syria including in the vicinity of Dier ez Zor, followed by a further wave of air strikes on north east Syria by the tactical aviation based at Hmeymim, followed by the cruise missile strikes launched by the Tu-160 and Tu-95MS, followed by a wave of air strikes on eastern Syria, probably in or around Dier ez Zor, by the tactical aviation based at Hmeymim, followed by a cruise missile strike launched from the Caspian Flotilla on eastern and North eastern Syria, followed by a second wave of cruise missiles launched from the Caspian Flotilla. This order of course may be subject to change in the event that more information is released by the MODRF.

FAB-250 series bombs, still in protective crates, being hoisted from storage before being loaded onto Tu-22M3 long range bombers during the period 16/17 November 2015. MODRF

In the early hours of the morning of Tuesday the 17th of November 2015, a force of twelve Tu-22M3 long-range bombers began to take off from Mozdok, the glow from their afterburning engines blazing a trail into the darkness of the night sky as the first long range bombing missions flown by Long Range Aviation in the Syrian campaign got underway. The bombers crossed the Russian North West coast of the Caspian Sea before turning southeastward, then onto a southwesterly course before crossing the southern Caspian coastline into northern Iran. Once in Iranian airspace the bombers continued on a southwesterly course that took them into northern Iraq before crossing into Syrian airspace and heading towards their targets in eastern Syria, flight range being in excess of 2000 km from their launch their base in North Ossetia.

Previous page: Air launched cruise missiles being loaded onto the rotary launcher in a weapons bay on a Tu-160. Above: FAB-250 series high explosive bombs being loaded onto a Tu-22M3 at Mozdok air base on 16 or 17 November 2015. MODRF

Over the course of 50 minutes, from 05.00 hours to 05.50 hours Moscow time (04.00 to 04.50 local time - Syria put its clocks back 1 hour on 30 October 2015) on the morning of 17 November, the 12 Tu-22M3's released their respective loads of FAB-250 series HE (High Explosive) bombs over targets in the provinces of Raqqah and Dier-ez-Zor; this latter town, which had been besieged by ISIS forces, would become a focus of future Tu-22M3 operations. Although the bombers were bathed in sunshine at their medium/high altitude, the target areas themselves were still in semi-darkness as sunrise in Dier ez Zor for example did not occur until 05.56 local time, the town having entered civil twilight at 05.29.

Previous page: Tu-22M3 long range bombers take-off from Mozdok air base in the early hours of 17 November 2015. Above: The two Tu-160s' take-off from Olenegorsk air base in the Kola Peninsula in the early hours of 17 November 2015. MODRF

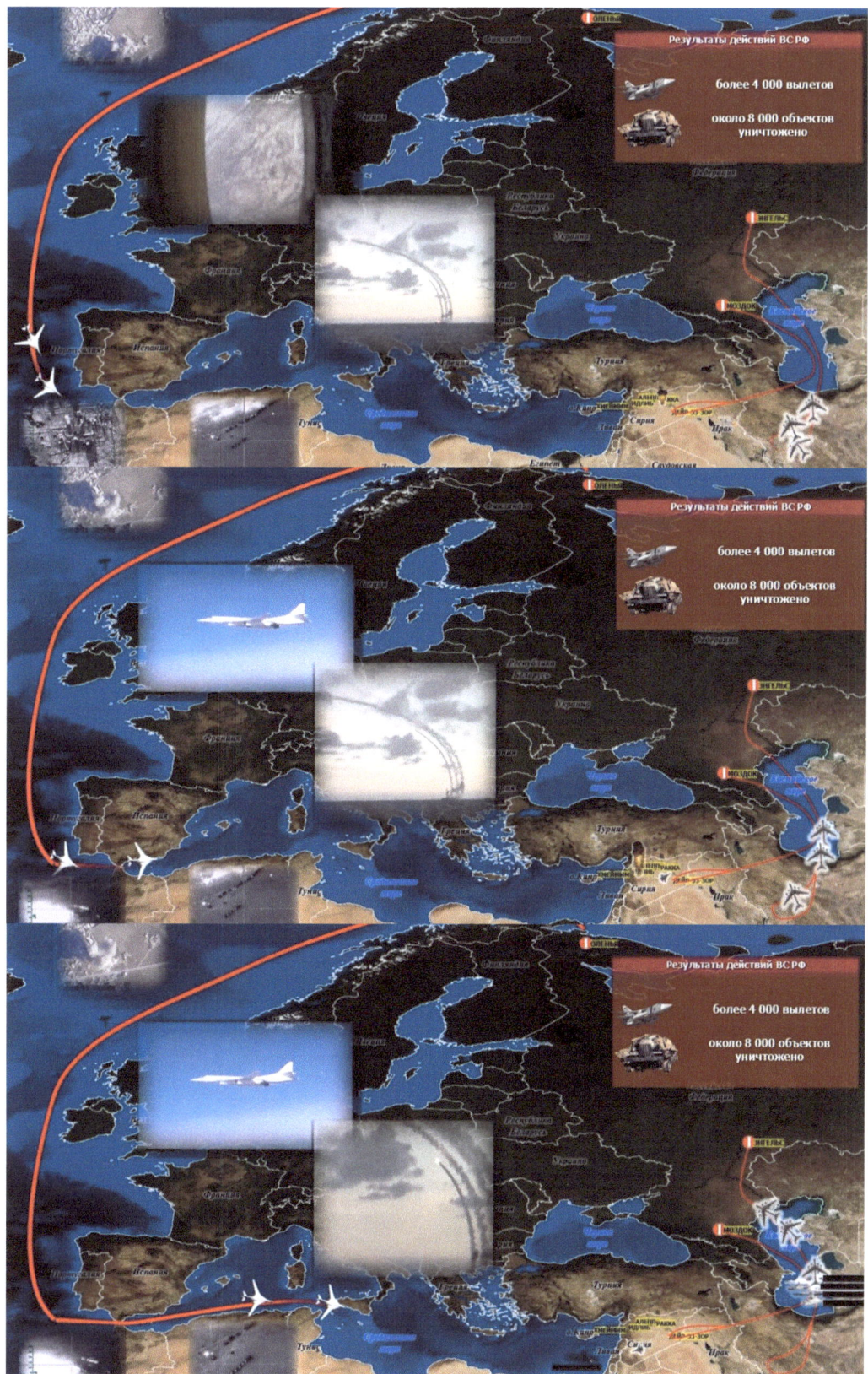

Page 48-51: **Frame 1** shows the Tu-160's taking-off from Olenegorsk in the Kola Peninsula, the Tu-22M3's transiting down the Caspian and tactical aviation over eastern Syria. **Frame 2** shows the Tu-22M3's bombing eastern Syria and the three Tu-95MS transiting down the Caspian. **Frame 3** shows the Tu-22M3's returning to base and the Tu-95MS launching missiles from Iranian airspace, the targets being struck in **frame 4** and **5**, with tactical aviation striking targets in eastern Syria in **frame 5**. **Frame 6** shows the Tu-95MS returning over the Caspian and cruise missiles being launched by the Caspian Flotilla, the targets being struck in **frame 7** and **8** along with targets being struck by missiles launched form the Tu-160 in **frame 8** and **9** and further cruise missiles form the Caspian Flotilla in **frame 10**, targets being struck in **frame 11** with the Tu-160's approaching Engels, Saratov. MODRF

In total six targets were bombed by the twelve Tu-22M3's, these being described by MODRF as "ammunition depots, weapons, clusters technology and training camps, workshops for the production of explosives". Once the bombs had been released the aircraft egressed the target areas then returned via northern Iraq, northern Iran and over the Caspian Sea before landing back at their start base, probably just before sunrise, which was timed as 07.57 am in Mozdok.

A few hours after the Tu-22M3's departed Syrian airspace the cruise missile carriers were preparing for their attack, comprising of two waves of missile carriers – one consisting of two Tu-160's from the 121st Guards Regiment flying out from Olenegorsk air base in the Kola Peninsula, northern Russia, and a second wave consisting of three Tu-95MS strategic missile carriers flying out from Engels air base, Saratov Oblast in Southern Russia, these thought to be from the resident 184th Guards Regiment.

Russia apparently requested permission for its Tu-160's to overfly certain European nations for the 17 November operation. However, this was unreservedly refused, throwing into question NATO's commitment to the fight against ISIS, despite agreement being reached at the (then) recent NATO summit that, as quoted by a UK MoD (Ministry of Defence) document, "ISIL [ISIS] constitutes a regional threat demanding a response including security and humanitarian assistance to those fighting ISIL on the front lines." However, within Russia, and the wider world these worlds appeared to ring hallow as NATO and other anti-ISIS coalition partners were in fact hindering, and in some cases, attacking the very forces embroiled in the fight against ISIS. While throwing their weight behind the so called moderate Syrian opposition, NATO and the wider coalition was in fact indirectly assisting ISIS by opposing the Syrian government forces, which was, and in early 2016, remained the only force on the ground in Syria with a the ability to defeat or at least roll back ISIS. Ironically, if Syrian government forces had collapsed under ISIS pressure prior to the Russian intervention this would have ultimately led to the collapse of the co-called moderate Syrian opposition, which would have been overwhelmed by superior ISIS forces released from the fight against government forces, pointing to a complete lack of strategic vision within the western dominated anti-ISIS coalition.

Tupolev Tu-22M3 bombers taxi at Mozdok prior to take-off (previous page) and take-off (above) in a series of video graphics shown as part of the 17 November operations, which would indicate that these aircraft were involved in the afternoon strike of twelve such aircraft armed with FAB-250 series (and possibly a few FAB-1500 series) high explosive bombs, as they are taking off during the hours of daylight. MODRF

The weapon bay of a Tu-22M3 with doors closed (top) and open just prior to bomb release (above). MODRF

With permission to overfly European nations refused, Russia took the opportunity to demonstrate its global strike capability – overflying European nations was not a necessity to its planned missions against targets in Syria. To this end the Tu-160's took off from Olenegorsk and transited down the Norwegian coast, passed to the north of the Orkney Islands swinging around Northern Scotland to the west of the Shetland Islands. As the bombers approached the UK air identification zone they were intercepted by RAF Eurofighter Typhoon fighters, which, according to the UK MoD, were scrambled from RAF Lossiemouth in what was portrayed as a dramatic interception of a potential violation of sovereign UK airspace.

Poor quality stills from MODRF video graphic media of the 17 November operations showing Tu-22M3's, escorted by two Su-30SM's, releasing their loads of FAB-250 series bombs (top) and a Tu-22M3, escorted by an Su-30SM dropping a single large weapon (centre and bottom). If authentic, there being no reason to assume otherwise as it was released by the MODRF, this indicates that the Tu-22M3's operated not only with the FAB-250 series 250 kg (500 lb.) class bombs, but also, on at least one occasion, a larger weapon, possibly the FAB-1500 series 1500 kg (3,300 lb.) class bomb. MODRF

Top: Twelve FAB-250 series bombs are released from the weapons bay of a Tu-22M3 (upper left of still) filmed from an external camera on an accompanying Tu-22M3. Above: Twelve FAB-250 series bombs are released from the weapons bay of a Tu-22M3 filmed from the crew compartment of an accompanying aircraft. MODRF

However, it is clear that the mission of the Tu-160's was already known to the UK government, which, along with the US and several other coalition partner nations such as France, had been informed of the mission prior to any of the Russian bombers taking off from their respective bases, this consideration being to reduce the possibility of misidentification. Despite this, in a remarkable statement that would allow the inference of this being an emergency scramble of interceptors to ward off a potential attack on Britain, the UK Defence Secretary Michael Fallon, in what came across as a prior prepared statement, said "RAF pilots have once again demonstrated their skill… This is another reminder that 24 hours a day, seven days a week, they are ready at a moment's notice to protect our skies." There was no mention that the times and routes of the Russian aircraft were prior known to the Ministry of Defence – in short it was not a QRA in the typical sense of the term, rather it was a pre-planned operation for RAF interceptors to positon themselves to shadow the Russian aircraft whilst near to the British area of interest.

Tu-22M3 Red 50 landing at Mozdok, North Ossetia, on 17 November 2015, following a bombing strike in the area of Dier ez Zor, Eastern Syria. MODRF

One of the Tu-160's with a shadow of two French fighter aircraft, apparently a Dassault Mirage 2000 and a Dassault Rafale. Crown Copyright

The British Typhoons shadowed the Tu-160's over the Atlantic Ocean heading southward, keeping well to the west of Ireland, at least two French fighters relieving the British fighters further south as the Russian bombers continued on their southward course towards the straits of Gibraltar. It should be noted that at no point did the Russian aircraft approach close to the UK mainland, remaining a considerable distance out in the Atlantic Ocean and they were considerably further at their closest approach to the French coast.

Once clear of the fighters the Tu-160's continued down the Atlantic Ocean keeping well to the west of the Iberian Peninsula, turning east through the straits of Gibraltar and over the western Mediterranean Sea before continuing eastward along the Mediterranean with the North African coastline to the south, past Sicily, keeping well to the south of the Island and then on towards the Eastern Mediterranean Sea keeping southward of Cyprus.

The Tu-95MS force took off from Engels, Saratov, Russia, crossed the north Caspian coastline and continued south easterly down the Caspian before turning to a south westerly course, crossing the southern Caspian coast into North Iran as the Tu-22M3 force was returning over North Iran and the Caspian Sea. While in Iranian airspace the Tu-95MS were, by prior arrangement with the Iranian government, escorted by Iranian Northrop Grumman F-14A Tomcat fighter aircraft as security against the unlikely scenario of third party nation interference with the operation.

As the Tu-160's neared the Syrian coast they were met by two Su-30SM fighter aircraft dispatched from Hmeymim air base, these escorting the bombers while over the eastern Mediterranean Sea and whilst they were in Syrian airspace.

Tu-160, RF-94113 (Red 17), launches a cruise missile against a target in Syria. MODRF

Over the course of forty minutes from 09.00 hours to 09.40 hours a total of 34 Kh-101 (as stated by the MODRF) air launched cruise missiles were released from Tu-160 and Tu-95MS carrier aircraft; these weapons being aimed at targets in Aleppo and Idlib. It appears that the two Tu-160's were the first to launch their missiles (conflicting with the charts above), 12 x Kh-101's being launched while off the Syrian Mediterranean coast (some graphic evidence suggest the possibility that the missiles were launched once landfall had been made) between 09.00 and 09.10 am, these being aimed at targets in Allepo and Idlib, North western Syria.

Previous page: Data released by the MODRF states that all air launched cruise missiles employed during the 17 November operations were Kh-101. However, while photographic and video data shows this may most likely the case for the weapons launched from the Tu-160, same photographic and video graphic data shows a completely distinct shape of weapon, resembling the Kh-55SM, being launched from the Tu-95MS, indicating that these weapons could be a conventional derivative of the Kh-55, often referred to as the Kh-555. Throwing further confusion on the account is the fact that the missile in the still at the top of page 60 and the missile in the still at the bottom of page 58 appear to be distinct from each other in regards to nose shape, both being distinct from the body shape of the missiles shown being loaded on a Tu-160 on page 44. MODRF This page: Tu-160's escorted, while in Syrian airspace, by Su-30SM 4th+ generation 'super-manoeuvrable' multirole fighter aircraft. MODRF

The three Tu-95MS launched 24 (MODRF figures) cruise missiles over Northern Iran, these apparently being aimed at targets in the Allepo and Idlib areas of western Syria. There is some ambiguity as to the numbers of weapons launched by each aircraft. As six is the maximum number that can be carried in the internal weapons bay of the Tu-95MS, it would appear that at least one of the aircraft was a Tu-95MS-16 which can carry an additional ten such missiles on underwing stations, this conveniently making up the required figure of 24 that was left over once the 12 missiles launched from the two Tu-160s was subtracted from the known figure of 34 air launched cruise missiles launched that day.

Top: A Tu-95MS during the 17 November 2015 operations against targets in Syria. MODRF. Above: A Tu-95MS being escorted by an Islamic Republic of Iran Air Force F-14A Tomcat fighter, apparently on 17 November 2015.

A total of 14 separate target areas were struck, including, according to the MODRF, "illegal armed groupings, which coordinated Islamic State troops in Idlib and Aleppo provinces; large depots of ammunition and other supplies located in protected shelters in the North West of Syria; terrorist training camps where reinforcements for terrorist units and suicide bombers were trained; three large factories manufacturing explosives, suicide vests and unguided rockets."

Following missile launch the three Tu-95MS retraced their route over northern Iran, the Caspian Sea and into southern Russia before landing back at their start base. The Tu-160 egress route was across Syria and into northern Iraq and then into North West Iran before turning to the northward over the Caspian Sea, continuing northwestward over the inland sea before crossing into Russian airspace and then on to Engels where, as noted above, the Tu-95MS also landed. It is unclear if the Su-30SM's escorting the Tu-160's continued into Northern Iraq, this being doubtful, but once the bombers were in Iranian airspace it is thought that they were met by Iranian fighter aircraft which provided close escort while in Iranian airspace.

The day's operations were not yet over for Long Range Aviation. A second Tu-22M3 bombing raid on targets in Eastern Syria was planned for the afternoon of the 17th. This mission, like the one that morning, being flown from Mozdok and consisting of twelve aircraft, all or most of which were apparently carrying 12 x FAB-250 series HE bombs (as previously noted, video graphic footage released by the MODRF shows at least one large weapon being released from a Tu-22M3, this thought to have been a FAB-1500 series bomb), which were released over a number of targets described by the MODRF as a "communications centre, an ammunition dump, mini-plants for the production of explosives and car bombs, as well as the training base". These Tu-22M3's followed, more or less, the same ingress and egress routes as the morning Tu-22M3 strikes, the aircraft still being airborne when the last of the cruise missiles carriers landed at Engels at 16.00 hours (probably Moscow Time), confirming that all of the cruise missile carriers had landed during the hours of daylight, the last of the Tu-22M3's from the afternoon strikes probably landing during civil twilight, sunset at Mozdok occurring at 17.35 hours local time.

During the course of the days bombing operation the Tu-22M3's covered distances of over 4000 km, one aircraft being in the air for 5 hours and 20 minutes during which it flew 4510 km. The Tu-95MS cruise missile carriers flew distances averaging 6566 km, being in the air on average 9 hours and 30 minutes. The Tu-160's covered distances estimated to be in excess of 8000 km, being in the air on average 8 hours and 20 minutes.

As well as the days operations by the missile carrier and bombers of Long Range Aviation, which consisted of 29 sorties, a further 98 sorties were flown by the tactical aviation assets of the Russian Aerospace Group based at Hmeymim. It is also known that eight Su-34 and 4 Su-27SM3 sorties were flown from southern Russia, the Suu-34's apparently being ferried to Hmeymim to reinforce the Russian Aerospace Group based there). There were also a number of support aircraft sorties flown such as those of the Il-78M in-flight refueling tanker aircraft which apparently refueled the Tu-160's over the Caspian Sea during the egress flight to Engels. In addition to the missile carrier, bomber and tactical aviation operations flown that day, although details are lacking, it seems that a number of Kalibr cruise missiles were launched form the small missile ships of the Caspian Flotilla, the numbers being unclear.

In a blow to Anglo-American political attempts to discredit the Russian Syrian campaign, 17/18 November saw France and Russia move closer together in their efforts to defeat ISIS, the Russian cruiser *Moskva* being ordered to make contact with and operate with the French naval group centred on the nuclear powered aircraft carrier, *Charles de Gaulle* then on passage to the coast of Syria to conduct operations against ISIS – the French and Russian deciding that petty political differences should not be allowed to obstruct their operations against ISIS in the wake of the destruction of a Russian airliner over Sinai on 31 October and the Paris terror attacks less than a week before, both attributed to ISIS – France, although publically united with its western partners within NATO, appearing more in line with Russia in regards to military goals in Syria – the defeat of ISIS.

Within days pf the Long Range Aviation cruise missile and bomb strikes tension between Russia and the NATO alliance increased exponentially following the shooting down of a Russian Su-24M strike aircraft over northern Syria by Turkish Lockheed Martin F-16 fighter aircraft on 24 November, in an action which could be inferred as a futile attempt by Turkey to force Russia to curtail operations near its borders, these geographical areas receiving particular attention from Russian strike and reconnaissance operations as Russia ramped up its strike and reconnaissance campaign against oil convoys and what Russia stated was a flow of ISIS fighters crossing the border from Turkey into Northern Syria.

Turkey claimed that the Russian aircraft crossed into Turkish airspace for 17 seconds, Russia denying this – that such a violation took place or not being largely academic as Turkey did not follow the accepted international rules for such incidents that do not allow nation states to simply open fire on aircraft that cross into their sovereign airspace. It is clear from the crash position, several km inside Syria, that the Su-24M was in Syrian airspace at the time of the attack – if moving away from the border there was no justification for an interception and if moving toward the border it must have been well within Syrian airspace before missile launch. The end result of Turkeys unprofessional action, considered a rash act of desperation in that nations confrontation with Russia, was the intensification of escort operations by Su-30SM fighter aircraft for Russian strike aircraft operating near the Turkish border, combined with the introduction of a sophisticated air defence system by the Russian Aerospace Group at Hmeymim, this consisting of a top tier S-400 Triumph SAM (Surface to Air Missile) system supported by short-range Pantsir-S2 systems. The S-400, with its extended range out to 400 km, effectively allowed Russia to control most of the Syrian airspace as well as potentially being capable of engaging aircraft in Turkish airspace, this adding no little insult to the Turkish government.

The net effect of the 24 November incident was that Russian strike aircraft, now protected by the Su-30SM fighters and under the cover of the S-400 missile systems, continued to operate near the Turkish border, and, for a while at least, the anti-ISIS coalition effectively abandoned operations over western Syria, this being claimed as a lack of available targets, but more realistically being accredited to a cooling period to allow tensions to subside before resuming operations, albeit on a small scale.

As it continued a high tempo of operations Russia had launched a further 18 Kalibr cruise missiles from the missile ships of the Caspian Flotilla on 20 November; seven separate target areas being struck in the Raqqa, Idlib and Aleppo districts, backing up the air operations of the Russian Aerospace Group which now stood at 69 combat aircraft., it appearing that the eight Su-34 strike aircraft and possibly the four Su-27SM3 fighter aircraft launched from southern Russia on 17 November had remained based at Hmeymim (the MODRF has not confirmed that Su-27SM3's were deployed to Syria, there being no visual evidence to back up unofficial statements to the contrary).

Following the shooting down of an Russian Su-24M strike aircraft by an AIM-9 Sidewinder infrared guided air to air missile launched by a Turkish F-16 fighter on 24 November 2015, Russia based a battery of long-range S-400 Triumph SAM systems at Hmeymim air base, allowing it to dominate the airspace over Syria, providing additional security to Russian aircraft operating over Syria. MODRF

December 2015 would be a busy month for the Tu-22M3 force based at Mozdok, a not inconsiderable number of sorties being flown against targets in Syria. At a MODRF briefing held on 25 December 2015, figures released showed that Long Range Aviation had flown 145 combat sorties with Tu-160 and Tu-95MS missile carriers and Tu-22M3 bombers since 17 November. No additional Tu-160 or Tu-95MS operations had been flown since the operations on 17 November, the burden of long range strike operations falling on the Tu-22M3 fleet. Deducting figures of 2 and 3 respectively for the number of Tu-160 and Tu-95MS sorties flown on 17 November left a balance of 140 sorties for the Tu-22M3 fleet, 24 of which it is known were flown on 17 November, leaving a new balance of 116 additional sorties that appeared to have been flown up to the date of the briefing, 25 December 2015.

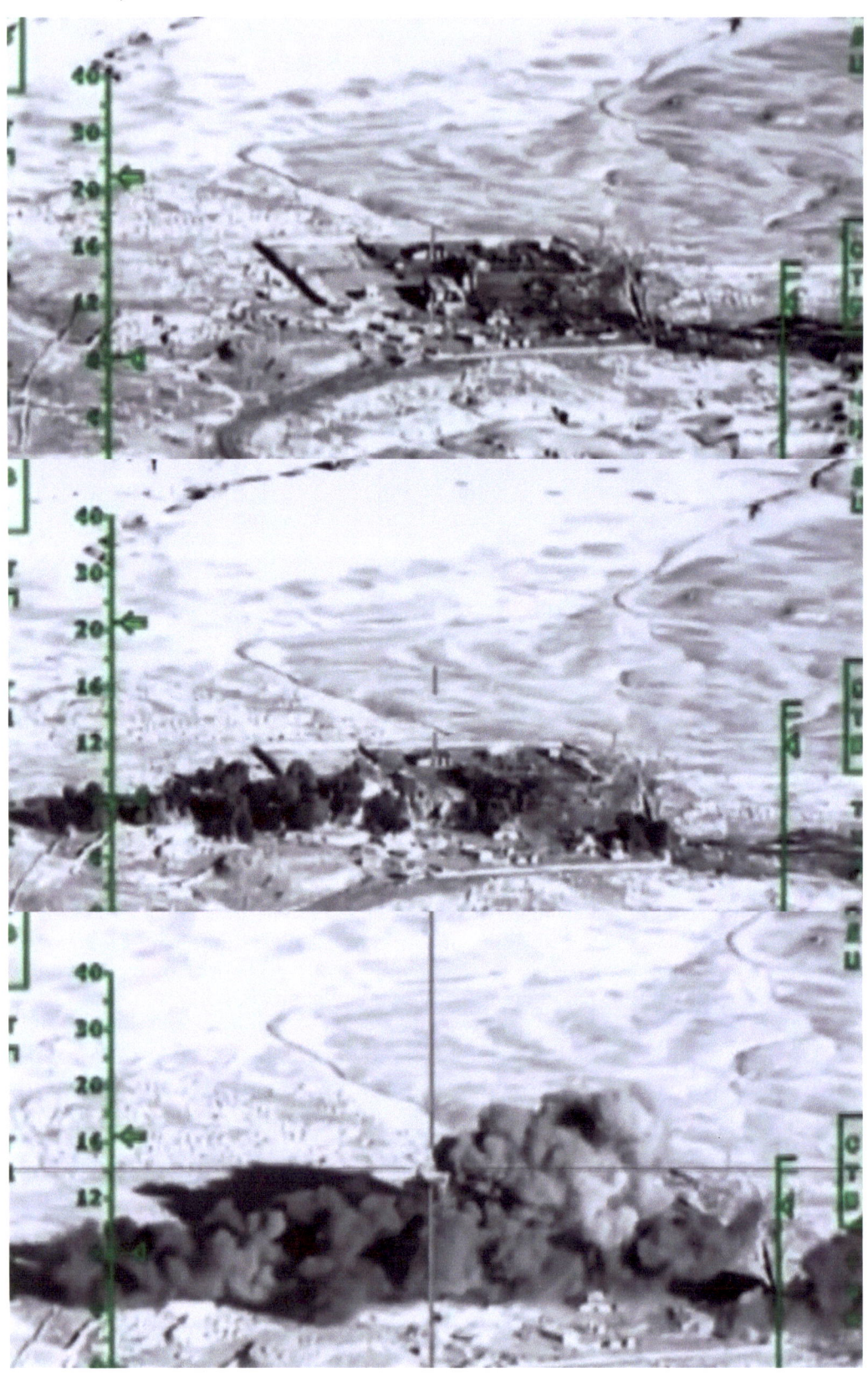

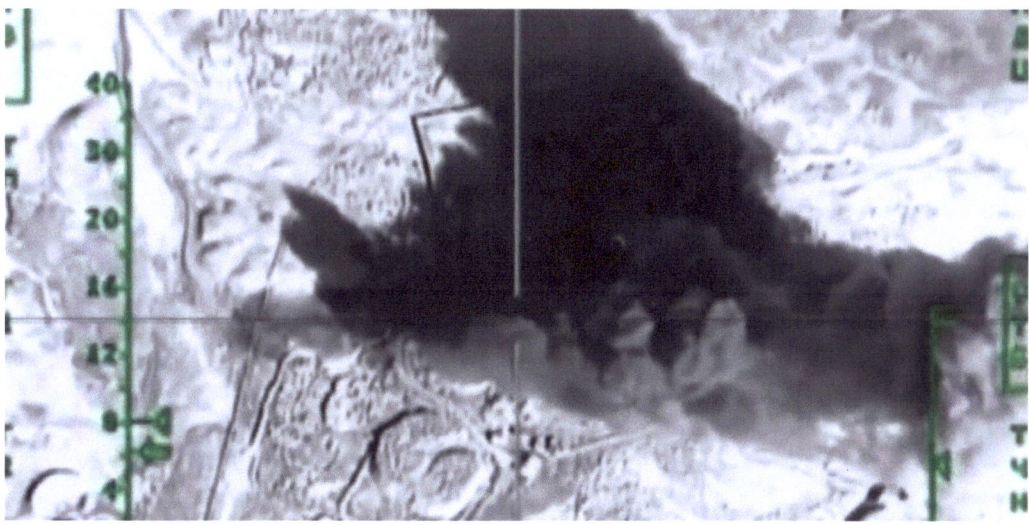

Page 66-67: Sequence of frames from a still from video taken from an UAV of a Tu-22M3 strike on a compound in eastern Syria, date unknown, with the basic description of a "terrorist base" by the MODRF. MODRF

It is clear from operational briefings that much of the Tu-22M3 effort was focused on the defence of the town of Dier ez Zor in eastern Syria which had been besieged for some time by ISIS forces. During the period of the first week in December a large number of Tu-22M3 sorties were flown against targets in Eastern Syria, mainly in or around Dier ez Zor; these attacks being on or after the 4th, the Russian defence minister stating on 8 December 2015 that the Tu-22M3 force had flown 60 combat sorties over the previous three days. Although released details are sparse, it is known that these Tu-22M3 operations, like the ones in November, were flown out of and recovered at Mozdok air base, North Ossetia. It is assumed that the ingress and egress routes were the same, or at least followed a similar route, to those of the 17 November missions.

The scene of the first Tu-22M3 strikes back in November, the region of the town of Dier ez Zor, was becoming particularly important to the Syrian government, and ultimately to the overall campaign against ISIS, being one of the few areas under government control outside western Syria, and the major area of government forces resistance in eastern Syria.

Having suffered setbacks in western Syria ISIS began planning a renewed offensive aimed at the capture of Dier ez-Zor, with the intention to overrun the defences and capture the town. While Syrian government forces were making significant gains in such areas as Northern Latakia, supported by the tactical aviation of the Russian Aerospace Group, ISIS was building up its forces in the area of Dier ez-Zor to support the forces laying siege to the town. Reinforcements apparently included 2000 fighters supported by armoured vehicles and other military hardware, which were withdrawn from other areas of Syria and concentrated near Dier ez Zor by the third week of January 2016.

Dier ez Zor, the surrounding area, controlled by ISIS, being a major target area in the Russian oil interdiction campaign as it was part of the transport route east to Mosul in Iraq, had become a focal point of tension between the US led coalition and Russia when the positions of Syrian government forces, the 168th Brigade of the 7th Division, tasked with the city's defence against ISIS, were attacked from the air some 2 km west of Dier over the course of 15 minutes commencing around 19.40 hours on the evening of 6 December 2015, leaving 4 killed and 12 wounded. Very quickly US Pentagon personnel apparently made statements, suggesting prior knowledge, that Russian aircraft had attacked the Syrian positions, but offering no evidence to support the claim. However, MODRF stated emphatically that no Russian aircraft were operating in that area at that time; this apparently being confirmed by Syrian air traffic control which monitored the Russian aircraft movements.

US representatives of the anti-ISIS coalition had been notified of all the Russian planned air operations at that time, none of which were over the area in question. According to the MODRF, the Pentagon confirmed that US aircraft were operating in that area at the time of the air strikes on 6 December, but that they struck targets some 55 km distant. These operations were known to the Russian Aerospace Group which was monitoring the US operations, but the MODRF stated that as well as the aircraft operating 55 km distant, two pairs of anti-ISIS coalition (nationality not stated) aircraft were operating over Dier ez-Zor at the time of the attack, these it being claimed as responsible for the attack on the Syrian 168th Brigade positions.

It is certainly true that the fall of Dier ez Zor would have been a significant setback for the Syrian government forces operating in central/East Syria, the supposition being that the western command structure was looking to loosen government forces control over parts of Syria even at the expense of assisting ISIS – in effect becoming de facto allies of the extremist organisation. When the actions of Turkey, positively hostile towards Russia, which was targeting opposition forces and oil transport convoys near the Turkish/Syrian border – Turkish F-16 fighters, as noted above, attacking and shooting down a Russian Su-24M strike aircraft on 24 November at the height of the oil interdiction campaign, are taken into consideration, then the picture that is painted appears to be one of misplaced priorities, any attempt to sneak in a jab at the Russian operations being taken. It certainly appears true that the US led coalition refrained, for the most part, from attacks on ISIS groups opposing Syrian government forces, completely calling into question its official label of the anti-ISIS coalition. Said coalition did however conduct attacks on ISIS targets that opposed the so called moderate opposition forces (funding and possibly, to a certain extent armed by same) , much of the illegal ISIS controlled oil producing and distribution resources, which Russia pointed out is transited through north Iraq and Turkey, generating billions of Dollars in illegal oil revenues, which constitutes the bulk of ISIS funding, being more or less left unmolested by the anti-ISIS campaign, a few minor strikes taking place, but the illegal oil pumping and distribution operation not being seriously targeted until the commencement of the Russian campaign – some 300 oil infrastructure targets being struck by Russian forces by late April 2016.

It should not be inferred that the US-led coalition supported an ISIS controlled Syria, but rather the misplaced priorities of the coalition have made it a pseudo policy for the overthrow of the Assad regime of the Syrian Arab Republic being of more importance than the defeat of ISIS, whereas the Russian view was that the Syrian government forces were the only force on the ground capable of bringing about the defeat of ISIS. The presumption being then that if ISIS defeated the government forces, then the US-led coalition could turn their unrestrained air power against ISIS in an attempt to destroy its forces, clearing the way for the so called moderate opposition forces to take control. All of this of course can be considered as conjecture, however, it remains clear that the anti-ISIS coalition air campaign had been completely ineffective as far as operations in Syria were concerned. A few notable success of targeted drone strikes being made public, but little to show on the ground for the effort expended. The effectiveness of the Russian campaign, which cannot be disputed by even the most ardent anti-Russian exponents, was due in no small part to the fact that the Russians knew exactly what their objectives were, striking targets mainly in support of a viable ground force able to make tactical advances and secure territory under the support of effective air support.

The fact that the Syrian Arab Republic army is, in early 2016, the only force on the ground capable of preventing a wholesale takeover of Syria by ISIS seems to be lost on western politicians more concerned with their own political agenda against Russia and the Assad regime than finding a way to end ISIS domination of much of Syria. It is hard to argue with the Russian view that its support for the Syrian government forces is, despite how disagreeable this may be to the pallet of many of the western powers, the best hope for defeating ISIS in Syria and ultimately in Iraq.

The seeds of the new Tu-22M3 assault on targets in the Dier ez Zor district of eastern Syria were sown in a Russian Presidential order of 5 December 2015, calling for an intensification of air and cruise missile attacks on ISIS and other factions Russia deemed to be terrorist organisation within Syria. This would result in further long range bombing and cruise missile strikes over the ensuing days, which, combined with an increased tempo of operations of the Russian Aerospace Group operating out of Hmeymim air base, resulted in around 300 sorties being flown during which in excess of 600 targets were struck, culminating with a cruise missile attack launched on the 8th of the month.

The 8 December cruise missile attacks deviated from the previous methods of using ship launched 3M-14T Kalibr or air launched cruise missiles. On this occasion 3M-14 missiles were launched form the torpedo tubes of the Russian Navy diesel electric Submarine *Rostov-on-Don* while the vessel was submerged in the Mediterranean Sea off the Syrian coast. This new vessel, commissioned earlier in 2015, was the second of six Project 636 Varshavyanka class submarines under order for the Russian Navy; these vessels being an evolution of the Russian Kilo Class diesel electric Submarine. The *Rostov-on-Don* apparently completed trials with the Russian Navy Northern Fleet in the Barents Sea in October 2015 and was apparently allocated to the Black Sea Fleet, it being assumed that her presence in the eastern Mediterranean Sea was related to her transfer to the Black Sea.

Top: The *Rostov on Don* Diesel electric submarine on the Surface in the eastern Mediterranean Sea, presumably prior to the 8 December cruise missile launches. Above: Two 3M-14 missiles already underway, a third has just broken the surface during the missile strike from the *Rostov on Don* on 8 December 2015. MODRF

The Kalibr missiles launched from the submarine were targeted at ammunitions storage facilities and at what was described as a mine production plant as well as elements of the oil producing and distribution infrastructure in the territory of Raqqah. Another report emanating from Russia stated that two ISIS command facilities were also struck. According to the MODRF all of the missiles hit the intended targets.

There is a fair degree of ambiguity surrounding the 8 December cruise missile strikes in regards to the numbers of missiles launched. MODRF statements indicate that 4 missiles were launched form the submarine, which being the case then some of the above mentioned targets sets would have had to have been in the same general vicinity so they could be destroyed by a single missile. Supporting the MODRF statements is video graphic footage showing no less than four missiles break the surface in the eastern Mediterranean Sea. Other, unconfirmed sources within the Pentagon stated that the submarine only launched a single missile, this clearly being inaccurate, and that at least ten more were launched by missile ships of the Caspian Flotilla, this claim having no evidence to support it.

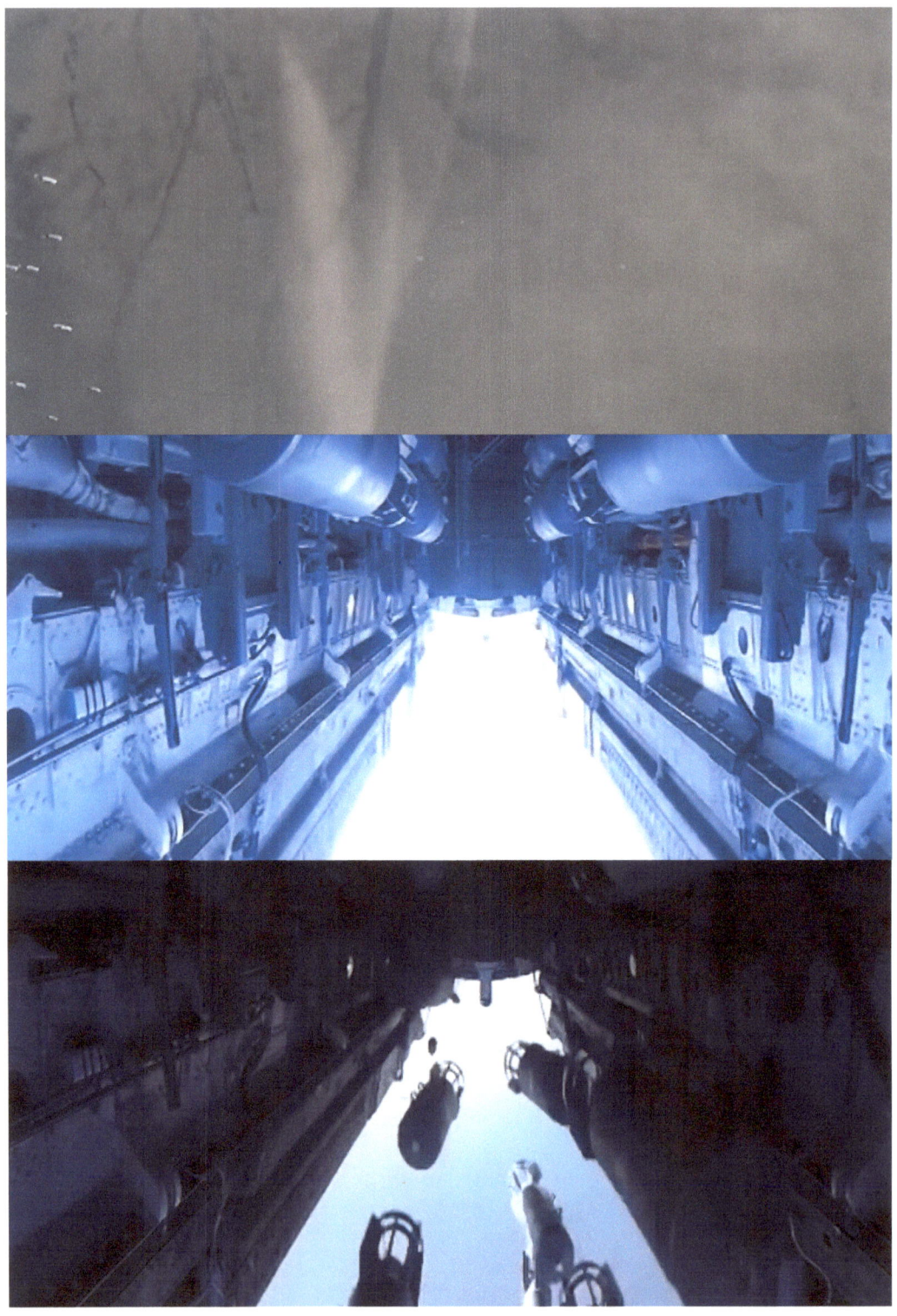

Page 71-72: Sequence of stills of bombs being released from the internal weapons bay of a Tu-22M3 and dropping towards the target. MODRF

Going into the New Year, the Syrian government forces continued to make progress on the ground, recapturing much land previously under ISIS control, particularly in Latakia. Dier ez Zor in the east was still under Siege, ISIS continuing to enforce its grip on the surrounding area. As noted above, in the third week of January 2016, new ISIS concentrations were discovered in the vicinity of Dier ez Zor by reconnaissance platforms resulting in tasking's for Russian aviation assets to attack the new threat to the town. As well as tactical strikes flown from Hmeymim by the Russian Aerospace Group, eighteen sorties were flown by Tu-22M3 bombers direct from Mozdok air base in southern Russia during the course of 22-24 January.

Page 73-74: Fish eye view from a weapon bay door camera showing FAB-250 series bombs stacked in rows of threes (the bombs are stacked vertical one above the other, the horizontal attitude in the first still being due to the angle of the camera), weapon bay doors opened and a FAB-250 series bomb dropping away from the weapon bay. MODRF

As fighting intensified, the besieged Dier ez-Zor was in dire need of humanitarian aid for its significant civil population, having been all but ignored by the international community which predominantly focused on areas occupied by the so called moderate Syrian opposition. To this end Syrian transport aircraft employed Russian P-7 parachute systems to drop in excess of 200 tons of essential supplies, mainly food and medicines, on the city during the course of January 2016.

In the last week of January the threat to the city remained grave as pressure increased on the ground defences requiring a high tempo of air operations to try and redress the situation. These air operations included further Tu-22M3 missions, 24 sorties being flown from Mozdok to bomb ISIS positions in the last week of January and possibly into the first day of February 2016. This close support to the Syrian army troops providing defence for Dier ez-Zor, in cooperation with tactical aircraft of the Aerospace Group operating from Hmeymim, which during the week flew some 468 sorties against targets not just in Dier ez Zor, but also against targets in eight separate Syrian Provinces, some 1,300 targets being struck. During the course of the operation in defence Dier ez Zor twenty three target areas were struck by the Tu-22M3's, contributing enormously to the defence of the city when it was being heavily assaulted by ISIS forces; the weight of the air strikes leading to the collapse of the ISIS offensive, casualties on the ground being in the hundreds on both sides, with no figures being available for civilian casualties caused by the ground fighting or indeed possibly as a result of air strikes.

The threat of intervention by the Turkish air force in northern Syria had largely been negated by the Russian Su-30SM fighters, which were joined by a small detachment of Su-35S multirole fighter aircraft, all backed by a modern air defence system centred on the S-400 long-range surface to air missiles previously noted, thus allowing the Russian Aerospace Group to dominate the airspace over most of Syria and even, had it been required, parts of Turkey and Iraq. The increased numbers of air defence fighters available allowed the Russian Aerospace Group to provide escorts as required, including for the Tu-22M3 operations emanating out of Russian territory, which, it is understood, were under the protection of Russian fighter aircraft while operating in Syrian airspace.

The campaign in defence of Dier ez Zor in late January was the swansong for the Long Range Aviation campaign over Syria which had commenced almost two and a half months before, government forces and 'moderate' opposition forces in Syria entering into a fragile cessation of hostilities on 27 February 2016. This first step towards peace, it has to be accepted, was made possible only by the Russian intervention, as prior to this the western powers were emphatic that there could be no peace talks until the Syrian President, Bashar al Assad, resigned. With the military support of Russia, the western governments were forced to accept the fact, no matter how unpalatable, that the moderate opposition that they had placed so much effort and money in backing, could not achieve the military objectives required to bring about a Syrian government collapse. The ascent of ISIS, which was all advancing in Syria prior to the Russian intervention, had placed the 'moderate' opposition into almost insignificance in the greater battle for Syria's future. The February cessation of hostilities (this has been shaky at best with many violations) being seen by many as the opposition groups best chance of having any meaningful part to play in Syria's future that neither side considers should include ISIS.

The path to peace in Syria, which will certainly be strewn with many obstacles, will only be possible if the Syrian people are allowed the right to self-determination free of outside political interference – compromises must be made on the Government/loyalist side and on the so called moderate opposition side if ISIS is defeated. To this end, in March 20016, Syrian government forces continued offensive operations against ISIS with one of the major goals being the intent to lift the siege of Dier ez Zor, the first stage being the liberation of the historic city of Palmyra, under the air support of the Russian Aerospace Group, from ISIS control which was accomplished towards the end of the month, a future aim being to try and force open the Palmyra to Dier ez Zor highway thus lifting the Siege.

By late-February 2016, the Russian Aerospace Group based at Hmeymim had flown in excess of 7,000 combat sorties since the commencement of its campaign on 30 September 2015. As far as can be ascertained Long Range Aviation flew 187 sorties (sorties were flown by Il-78M tanker aircraft, it being less than clear whether the figure of 187 sorties includes tanker aircraft sorties or refers purely to offensive sorties) during the campaign. Of these totals, 2 sorties were flown by Tu-160's, 3 by Tu-95MS leaving a balance of 182 for the Tu-22M3, 126 sorties of which can be accounted for. It is possible that the figure of 187 sorties may actually include sorties flown by support aircraft as mentioned above, attempts to have this confirmed or refuted by the MODRF proving unsuccessful. Supporting this hypothesis is a MODRF statement that 1500 FAB-250 bombs had been deployed, the figure of 126 known Tu-22M3 sorties calculating at 1512 FAB-250 bombs, assuming a load of twelve such weapons on each sortie. However, this figure was released by the MODRF prior to the late January operations flown by the Tu-22M3 fleet. If the Tu-22M3 sortie numbers were as high as the figure of 182 previously mentioned, then, at a load of 12 FAB-250 bombs per sortie, total numbers of FAB-250 bombs deployed by the Tu-22M3 fleet would be 2184, assuming of course that all weapons were dropped. There is of course another variable to be considered, that being that video graphic evidence indicates that at least one and possibly more larger weapons, probably FAB-1500 class weapons, were dropped by the Tu-22M3 force, this probably slightly reducing the overall numbers of FAB-250 series weapons deployed.

The five sorties flown by the Tu-160 and Tu-95MS – 2 and 3 respectively – deployed, according to the MODRF, 34 Kh-101 cruise missiles (as previously noted there appear to be distinct differences in the types of cruise missiles employed by the Tu-95MS and Tu-160) to which can be added 63 Kalibr cruise missiles launched by the missile ships of the Caspian Flotilla and the *Rostov-on-Don* Submarine.

By contrast, by late February 2016, the US-led anti-ISIS coalition, which commenced bombing operations over Syria on 22 September 2014, more than a year before the commencement of the Russian campaign, had flown only some 3500 sorties over Syria, a mere 30 of which had been flown by the RAF since the high profile commencement of the British campaign, which can be considered to be more a political gesture than a serious military operation, on 3 December 2015, almost three months before, equating to roughly one sortie every three days for the British operation. The campaign had had little effect on the ground, in part because the anti-ISIS coalition would not target ISIS units opposing Syrian government forces, which constituted the bulk of ISIS military power in Syria, targeting being focused on ISIS forces opposing the so called moderate opposition, vastly reducing the scale of tactical target sets available. The illegal ISIS oil infrastructure, as previously noted, had been left to a large extent unmolested until the Russian campaign stepped up pressure on the production and distribution infrastructure, particular anger being voiced in Moscow over the appearance of NATO nation collusion in the illegal distribution of the oil, which Russia contended is sold through Turkey.

On the strategic stage, the political leadership in Washington and London were gradually forced to cede their position to one of supporting cast, in the UK almost to one of bystander, as Russia, having taken the initiative in the Syrian campaign, following a disastrous several months in which Syrian government forces had lost just under 20 percent of land to ISIS and other opposition groups, provided the support required to allow the Syrian Arab Republic Army to begin to roll back ISIS. The western powers hopes for a united Syrian opposition, funded mainly by Washington, having been abandoned as the so called moderate opposition and its anti-ISIS coalition air support were forced to cede to a tertiary position within Syria and take the roadmap to peace that, as noted above, had previously been rejected as unacceptable unless the Syrian President first resigned.

APPENDICES

Appendix I

Tupolev Tu-22M3 Long-Range Bomber/Missile Carrier

Engines: Two NK-25 three-stage afterburning turbofans each rated at 25000 kgf (Height=0, Mach=0, ISA) with a specific fuel consumption at take-off of 2.08 kg/kgf/h
Length: 42.46 m
Height: 11.05 m
Wing span: 34.28 m at 20° sweep and 27.70 m at 65° sweep
Maximum take-off weight: 124 tons (124000 kg)
Normal combat load: 12000 kg
Maximum combat load: 24000 kg
Maximum speed: 2000 km/h
Cruising speed: 900 km/h
Service ceiling: 14000 m
Tactical range: 2200 km
Take-off run: 2000-2100 m
Landing roll: 1200-1300 m
Crew: Four – pilot, co-pilot, navigator and systems operator

Appendix II

Tupolev Tu-95MS Strategic Missile Carrier

Engine: 4 x HK-12M each generating 15,000 hp for a combined power output of 60,000 hp
Length: 49.13 m
Height: 13.3 m
Wing span: 50.4 m
Wing sweep position in the line of ¼ chord: 35°
Maximum take-off weight: ~187 tons
Maximum speed: 830 km/h
Service ceiling: 10500 m
Ordnance: Tu-95MS-6 can carry 6 Kh-55 or Kh-102 nuclear armed long-range cruise missiles or six conventional armed cruise missiles carried on a rotary launcher housed in the internal weapons bay. The Tu-95MS-16 can carry six cruise missiles on a rotary launcher in the internal weapons bay and 10 on under wing stations on the inner wing sections
Crew: Up to seven

Appendix III

Tupolev Tu-160 Strategic Missile Carrier/Bomber

Engines: 4 x NK-32 turbofan engines each rated at 25 tons (~22680 kg) in afterburner
Length: 54.10 m
Height: 13.2 m
Wing span: 55.7 m at 20° sweep, 50.7 m at 35° sweep and 35.6 m at maximum sweep back of 65°
Wing sweep position in the line of ¼ chord: 35°
Maximum take-off weight: 275000 kg (275 tons)
Maximum speed: 1800 km/h (Kret lists speed as 2000 km/h, this being unlikely)
Cruise speed: ~1030 km/h
Service ceiling: 14000 m
Range: ~14000 km maximum unrefueled or 10000 km with maximum ordnance.
Ordnance: 22500 kg (Kret figures state 40000 kg maximum)
Crew: Four - pilot, co-pilot, navigator and systems operator

Appendix IV

OKB Novator Kalibr-NK 3M-14T/3M-14

Engine: one NPO Saturn 36MT rated at 450 kgf maximum thrust
Range: ~2000 km
Operational altitude: 30 m and upwards
Flight profile: dependent upon terrain to be overflown
Warhead type: conventional and nuclear
Warhead weight: 500 kg class
Accuracy: Within 5 m
Launch platforms: Surface warships (3M-14T) and submarines (3M-14)
Vessels known to have launched missiles during the Syrian campaign include the project 11661K Gepard Class Frigate, *Dagestan*, the Project 21631 small missile ships (Buyan Class Corvette) *Grad Sviyazhsk*, *Veliky Ustyug* and *Uglich* and the Project 636 Varshavyanka class submarine *Rostov on Don*

Appendix V

JSC Tactical Missiles Corporation (JSC Raduga State Engineering Design Bureau) Kh-101
Cruise speed: Unknown but thought to be similar to the Kh-55 ~850 km/h **Operational altitude:** 30 m and upwards **Range:** In excess of 4500 km (MODRF figure) **Flight profile:** dependent upon terrain to be overflown **Warhead type:** Conventional **Warhead weight:** thought to be 500 kg class **Accuracy:** Within 5 m **Carrier:** Tupolev Tu-95MS and Tu-160

Appendix VI

Long Range Aviation Tu-22M3's known to have flown operational sorties against targets in Syria during the November 2015 - February 2016 campaign

Tu-22M3	Serial number	Bort Code
	RF-94142	
	RF-94157	Red 28
	RF-94216	Red 26
	RF-94233	Red 20
		Red 16
		Red 24
		Red 37
		Red 42
		Red 46
		Red 48
		Red 50
		Red 57

Note: The MODRF has only acknowledged a Regiment of twelve Tu-22M3's as having operated from Mozdok during the campaign, however, it is possible that additional aircraft rotated in and out of the inventory of the Regiment based there

GLOSSARY

APU	Auxiliary Power Unit
B	Bomber
DBS	Doppler Beam Sharpening
ECM	Electronic Counter Measures
F	Fighter
GLONASS	Globanaya Navigozionnaya Sputnikovaya Sistema (Global Navigation Satellite System)
GPS	Global Positioning System
HF	High Frequency
ICBM	Intercontinental Ballistic Missile
INS	Inertial Navigation System
IR	Infrared
ISIL	Islamic State of Iraq and the Levant (also known as ISIS or Daesh)
ISIS	Islamic State (also known as ISIL or Daesh)
JSC	Joint Stock Company
kg	Kilogram
kgf	Kilogram Force
kg/kgf/h	Kilogram/kilogram force per hour
km/h	Kilometer per hour
lb.	Pound (measure of weight)
LRA	Long Range Aviation
m	Metre (measure of length/distance)
M	Modernised
Mach	(Speed of Sound)
MAWR	Missile Approach Warning Receiver
MOD	Ministry of Defence
MODRF	Ministry of Defence of the Russian Federation
MR	Modernised Reconnaissance
NATO	North Atlantic Treaty Organisation
NAVSTAR	Navigation Satellite Timing and Ranging System
PAK DA	Perspective [Prospective] Aviation Complex for Long Range Aviation
PAK FA	*Perspektivniy Aviacionniy Complex Frontovoi Aviacii* – Perspective [Prospective] Aviation Complex for Front line Aviation
PJSC	Public Joint Stock Company
POL	Petroleum Oil Lubricants
QRA	Quick Reaction Alert
RAF	Royal Air Force
RWR	Radar Warning Receiver

SAM	Surface to Air Missile
SAR	Synthetic Aperture Radar
SLBM	Submarine Launched Ballistic Missile
SM	Serial Modernised
Su	Sukhoi
TFR	Terrain Following Radar
Tu	Tupolev
UAC	United Aircraft Corporation
UAE	United Arab Emirates
UAV	Uninhabited Air Vehicle
UHF	Ultra-High Frequency
UK	United Kingdom
US	United States
USAF	United States Air Force
x	Times (multiplication)
~	Approximately equal to (can also be used to mean asymptotically equal)
°	Degree (angle)

ABOUT THE AUTHOR

Hugh, a historian and author, has published in excess of sixty books; non-fiction and fiction, writing under his given name as well as utilising two different pseudonyms. He has also written for several international magazines, whilst his work has been used as reference for many other projects ranging from the aviation industry, international news corporations and film media to encyclopaedias, museum exhibits and the computer gaming industry. He currently resides in his native Scotland

Other titles by the author include

Sukhoi T-50/PAK FA - Russia's 5th Generation 'Stealth' Fighter
Sukhoi Su-35S 'Flanker' E - Russia's 4++ Generation Super-Manoeuvrability Fighter
Sukhoi Su-34 'Fullback'
Sukhoi Su-30MKK/MK2/M2 - Russo Kitashiy Striker from Amur
MiG-35/D 'Fulcrum' F – Towards the Fifth Generation
Eurofighter Typhoon - Storm over Europe
Tornado F.2/F.3 Air Defence Variant
Air to Air Missile Directory
North American F-108 Rapier - Mach 3 Interceptor
Convair YB-60 - Fort Worth Overcast
Boeing X-36 Tailless Agility Flight Research Aircraft
X-32 - The Boeing Joint Strike Fighter
X-35 - Progenitor to the F-35 Lightning II
X-45 Uninhabited Combat Air Vehicle
Into The Cauldron - The Lancaster MK.I Daylight Raid on Augsburg
Light Battle Cruisers and the Second Battle of Heligoland Bight
British Battlecruisers of World War 1 - Operational Log, July 1914-June 1915
Hurricane IIB Combat Log - 151 Wing RAF, North Russia 1941
RAF Meteor Jet Fighters in World War II, an Operational Log
Typhoon IA/B Combat Log - Operation Jubilee, August 1942
Defiant MK.I Combat Log - Fighter Command, May-September 1940
Blenheim MK.IF Combat Log - Fighter Command Day Fighter Sweeps/Night Interceptions, September 1939 - June 1940
Tomahawk I/II Combat Log - European Theatre, 1941-42
Fortress MK.I Combat Log - Bomber Command High Altitude Bombing Operations, July-September 1941
F-84 Thunderjet - Republic Thunder
USAF Jet Powered Fighters - XP-59-XF-85
XF-92 - Convairs Arrow

www.ingramcontent.com/pod-product-compliance
Lightning Source LLC
Chambersburg PA
CBHW040058160426
43192CB00003B/108